Everyday Mindfulness

*108 Simple Practices to Empower Yourself
and Transform Your Life*

Melissa Steginus

ISBN: **978-1-63161-082-0**

Published by TCK Publishing
www.TCKpublishing.com

Get discounts and special deals on books at
www.TCKpublishing.com/bookdeals

This book comes with free mindfulness resources, worksheets, and exercises to help you transform your life. Get your resources at
www.melissasteginus.com/mindful

Sign up for Melissa Steginus' newsletter at
www.melissasteginus.com/subscribe

For anyone who wants to live with greater awareness and intention.

TABLE OF CONTENTS

INTRODUCTION

WHAT IT MEANS TO BE MINDFUL

Mindfulness is about paying attention with intention. Powerful things happen when you take a moment to fully observe your thoughts, feelings, behaviors, and surroundings. You begin to recognize what it means to be alive—to think, to feel, to exist in an infinite universe filled with infinite possibilities. When you give your full attention to the world around you and the one within you, you gain a deep appreciation for your existence, and you learn how to access the profound insights and wisdom you hold. You expand your consciousness, or rather, you tap into the full consciousness that already lies within you.

To be mindful is to embody this consciousness, to live your life in accordance with the realization that you're alive. This process doesn't have to be revolutionary. In fact, as you cultivate the simple yet profound practice of paying attention, most days might feel quite ordinary. This is because the transformative power of mindfulness lies in practice. You can use your daily tasks and routines to immerse yourself in the present moment and appreciate the wonder of your existence—if you pay attention.

This book contains insights and exercises designed to help you cultivate mindfulness in all areas of your life. Slowly and with everyday practice, you will come to appreciate your existence, connect with your inner wisdom, and tap into your capacity for self-empowerment, fulfillment, and transformation.

As you work through this book, your practice will center on and strengthen two areas of focus: self-empowerment and personal fulfillment.

EMPOWERMENT:

Practicing mindfulness will lead you to the depths of self-awareness. Through observation, interaction, and regular reflection, you have the power to connect with yourself and the world around you. You will explore your worthiness, the beauty of your existence, and your unlimited capacity to create meaningful changes in your life.

FULFILLMENT:

With awareness and connection as your foundation, you will step into (or create, if you prefer) a fuller, more complete version of yourself. You will get to know yourself on a real, intimate level and tune in to the powerful wisdom and potential you hold deep inside of you. Through empowerment, you will learn about and believe in your capacity and inner resources; through fulfillment, you will use them.

You already have the inner resources you need to empower yourself, cultivate fulfillment, and transform your life, but you have to do the work to recognize and tap into these resources and your potential. That's what this book and these next 108 days are all about.

THE SIGNIFICANCE OF 108

You've probably heard that it takes 21 days to build a habit, so you may be wondering why on earth we're looking at 108 days. After all, that's fifteen weeks or nearly four months!

First of all, this book is not about stacking a big, daunting habit onto your routine (like hitting the gym at 5 a.m. every day for three weeks). Mindfulness is a mindset and lifestyle shift that occurs through simple, regular practices (like tuning in to your breath or taking time to be creative). It takes time to shift into a mindful mindset, and giving yourself 108 days of practice instead of 21 will provide you with much more guidance, support, and confidence over the next four months and for the rest of your life.

But the meaning behind the number 108 extends far beyond its numerical value. So what makes it so special? To answer that question, let's zoom out for a moment and take a look at the cosmos:

- The diameter of the sun is 108 times the diameter of the earth.

- The diameter of the sun multiplied by 108 equals the miles between the sun and earth.

- The diameter of the moon multiplied by 108 equals the miles between moon and earth.

Therefore, it's believed by some that there are 108 steps between ordinary human awareness and the divine truth at the center of our being.

In addition, if we consider the visual symbolism of the number 108, we see:

1 = higher power or ultimate truth
0 = wholeness of self or existence
8 = infinity

Not only does this number hold its weight in calculating our planet's connection to the sun—the source of energy and life on Earth—but it also represents our complete and infinite existence in accordance with our truth. The number 108 holds incredible significance on both individual and cosmic levels; it represents completion, or the whole of existence, and that is exactly what I want for you throughout these 108 days and beyond. My hope is for you to become your fullest, truest self; to connect with the world and wonderful people around you; and to step into your life so you begin to actively create an existence that fulfills you.

HOW TO USE THIS BOOK

The beauty of this book is that it works with the things you probably do all the time. All you have to do is keep doing your thing—but with a little extra attention. So instead of 21 days of hustling to build a totally new habit, you've got 108 days to gradually train your brain to pay closer attention to activities and practices you may already be familiar with (i.e., deep breathing, journaling, self-reflection, goal-setting, etc.).

This slow and steady approach allows you to explore simple practices in small doses so you can find what works for you. Pay attention to what you enjoy or what strikes a chord with you so you can continue those practices past day 108. Be sure to dog-ear those pages and mark up this book as much as you want!

HOW IT WORKS:

Your next 108 days are divided into six sections. Each section represents a facet of you as a person.

1. Physical: Listening to your body and reconnecting with yourself
2. Emotional: Understanding your feelings and learning to trust them
3. Rational: Observing your thought patterns to gain mental clarity
4. Spiritual: Exploring your relationship with yourself and your truth
5. Occupation: Managing your time and energy to pursue your priorities
6. Network: Nourishing relationships that deepen your sense of belonging

Within each section, there are 18 exercises that will help you explore that particular facet. Every practice contains an explanation about the purpose behind the practice, your exercise for the day, and a few reflection questions. Each morning, when you open your book to the corresponding day, you'll read the day's practice and learn about its benefits. Give yourself a moment to think about how and when you'll do your practice, and schedule it into your day.

Each exercise is structured to be quick and simple enough to integrate into your day so you won't need to set aside an hour to try something totally new (unless you want to, of course). Commit to yourself each day by showing up and doing the work. Give each exercise your full attention so you can find what resonates with you and witness its impact on your life.

Once you've completed the day's exercise, return to your book and reflect. There are a few questions with every practice to guide you through your reflection. Take a few minutes right after you've done your practice to respond to each prompt, and jot down any other thoughts, questions, and answers as they arise. You can also do the reflection piece of your process in the evening if you have a bedtime journaling routine. Whatever your choice, make sure you participate in this important step so you can keep track of what you've learned, how you've grown, and what you might want to practice again in the future.

To recap, here is your step-by-step process for the next 108 days:

1. Open your book to the corresponding day.
2. Learn about the practice for that day.
3. Do each exercise with full attention and intention. (You might do this right away, or at some point later on in your day.)
4. Return to your book and reflect. (You can do this either immediately after your practice or right before bed. Write in these pages or use a separate journal if you prefer).

And when your 108 days are up: reflect, rejoice, and redo any or all practices as many times as you like!

HOW TO GET THE MOST OUT OF THIS BOOK:

1. Commit to 108 days.

The actions you take as you move through this book have the potential to change the rest of your life—but they won't if you just flip to a random page, read the title, and call it a day. Commit to investing your time and energy into the practice of mindfulness by going through the steps above every day. By being open, engaged, and consistent, you have the power to transform the next 108 days and beyond.

2. Take things day by day.

While I appreciate exploration and spontaneity, I've organized this book with careful intention and I encourage you to follow the days in order. This will help you maintain consistency and flow smoothly through each section, as certain days will build on previous lessons or exercises.

3. Reflect on your journey.

Whether you do this step right after your practice or just before bed, make sure to give yourself the time and space to think honestly about each question. Write your answers in these pages or use sticky notes or a separate journal if you intend to reuse this book (which you certainly can!).

Mindful tip: If you choose to do your reflection right after your practice, take a few minutes before bed to review what you wrote. Doing so allows you to see how your practice impacted your day and fosters the beautiful habit of recognizing your actions and celebrating your growth.

COMMIT TO YOURSELF

The next 108 days will require you to take an active role in your life to become more aware, empowered, and fulfilled. You won't gain mindfulness by passively sitting around and waiting for it to fall into your lap. You are now holding 108 simple and wonderful practices that will enrich your body, mind, soul, work, and relationships. Now it's up to you to do the work.

The actions you take over the course of this book are an investment in the rest of your life. You are committing to a new, more intentional way of being which can transform your relationship with yourself and enrich the way you live your life. Use the lessons and practices in this book to build the foundation for your personal, powerful, and ongoing transformation.

Remember that you have the capacity for your empowerment, fulfillment, and transformation. You are capable of tapping into this potential—and you deserve to. As you awaken to this reality and grow to accept it, you will quiet the voice that tells you otherwise.

Here are my three wishes for you (which you deserve and are capable of):

1. May you recognize your worth and live according to it.
2. May you truly appreciate the beauty of your existence.
3. May you trust in your ability to create fulfilling changes in your life and yourself.

This is what you'll need to commit to:

1. Be open to exploring different facets of your life and yourself.
2. Be willing to try each exercise to find what will work for you.
3. Be patient with yourself as you awaken and connect to all that is within you.

Finally, to set your intentions before you begin, say the following mantras aloud:

- "I am open to exploring who I am."
- "I will practice mindfulness every day."
- "I promise to be patient with myself."
- "I am ready to connect to all that is within me."

Now it's time to step into the wisdom within and awaken, empower, and fulfill your true self.

RESOURCES:

This book comes with free mindfulness resources, worksheets, and exercises to help you transform your life. Get your resources at: **www.melissasteginus.com/mindful**

CHAPTER ONE: PHYSICAL

"The body itself is to reveal the light that's blazing inside your Presence."

—RUMI

DAY 1

TAKE A DEEP BREATH

PURPOSE:

Deep breathing connects you to your body, mind, and the present moment. This practice reduces stress and tension, relieves body aches and pain, lowers blood pressure, and aids in healthy sleep.

PRACTICE:

Sit tall in a comfortable chair and plant your feet firmly on the ground. Pull your shoulders back and place both hands on your abdomen. Inhale deeply through your nose, filling your lungs and feeling your abdomen expand. Exhale through your mouth and feel your abdomen slowly release. Close your eyes and take five deep breaths.

REFLECTION:

How did you feel while doing this breathing exercise?

How did you feel afterward?

How did this practice make you more aware of your body?

DAY 2

GET A GOOD NIGHT'S SLEEP

PURPOSE:

A good night's sleep contributes to a healthy body, clear mind, and stable emotions. It also betters your memory and learning capabilities, allowing you to pay attention, make decisions, solve problems, and be creative.

PRACTICE:

Whatever your schedule and sleep patterns, aim for eight hours of consecutive rest tonight. Prepare your mind and body for rest with a relaxing evening routine (even if it's a few minutes of light stretching or five deep breaths). Do what you can to minimize distractions and make your room as dark as possible.

REFLECTION:

How many hours of sleep do you usually get?

How do you normally feel when you wake up?

NEXT MORNING:

How did you feel after a full night's rest?

DAY 3

MAKE AND EAT BREAKFAST

PURPOSE:

Breakfast provides the body and brain with fuel after an overnight fast ("break-fast"). Eating a healthy meal in the morning energizes you by kickstarting your metabolism, and it can also lead you to make healthier food choices throughout the day.

PRACTICE:

Give yourself enough time in the morning to prepare and eat a healthy breakfast (prep the night before if you need to). Set aside your phone and spend time being mindful of what you're consuming to fuel yourself for your day.

REFLECTION:

How did it feel to slow down and eat breakfast?

How might eating a healthy breakfast impact your relationship with food?

How might this practice help you set yourself up for a mindful day?

DAY 4

DRINK PLENTY OF WATER

PURPOSE:

Staying hydrated is crucial to maintaining the function of every system in your body. It detoxifies your organs, boosts your mental focus and physical performance, and prevents all kinds of pains and ailments.

PRACTICE:

You may have heard the recommendation to drink around eight cups of water each day. Try boosting your water intake today by keeping a water bottle with you and refilling it halfway through your day. Toss in some lemon or cucumber slices for flavor, and remind yourself to hydrate with a note on your desk or by setting hourly reminders on your phone.

REFLECTION:

How does your body feel when you are hydrated?

Why is it important to you to give your body what it needs?

DAY 5

RELEASE TENSION

PURPOSE:

Listening to and connecting with your body can transform your relationship with yourself. Activities like stretching, yoga, and massage can help alleviate stress, prevent tension and injuries, and increase mobility while practicing self-nourishment.

PRACTICE:

Explore the practice of progressive muscle relaxation to ease your body and mind.

1. Practice this technique while lying down comfortably with a pillow under your knees.
2. Take a few slow, deep breaths, inhaling through your nose and exhaling through your mouth.
3. Clench your hands into fists. Hold as tightly as you can for five seconds, then slowly release as you exhale. Remember to continue your deep breathing.
4. Focus on how it feels when you let go.
5. Repeat steps 2 to 4, contracting and releasing the muscles in each part of your body. Start with your feet, and work your way up through your calves, thighs, glutes, lower back, abdomen, hands, arms, shoulders, jaw, and face.

REFLECTION:

What sensations did you notice in your body during this practice?

How did this progressive relaxation help you release tension?

How did it help you connect with your body?

DAY 6

PRACTICE GOOD POSTURE

PURPOSE:

Good posture keeps your bones and joints properly aligned, preventing muscle pain and fatigue and keeping your spine strong and healthy. It also builds your confidence as you stand tall, appear composed, and feel healthier and more comfortable in your body.

PRACTICE:

Sit in a chair and practice one deep breath. Relax your shoulders (so they aren't up by your ears) and gently draw them toward your spine. Look straight ahead, keeping your neck neutral. And smile because you look great!

Check your posture at least once every half hour and repeat this practice as necessary.

REFLECTION:

How does good posture feel in your neck, shoulders, and back?

Where does it relieve tension?

How might good posture affect your attention span or confidence?

DAY 7

DO A WALKING MEDITATION

PURPOSE:

Mindful or meditative walking involves deliberately thinking about a series of actions you normally do on autopilot. This encourages you to be attentive to both the outside world and yourself more regularly. Compared to traditional seated meditation, many people find walking to be easier and more enjoyable. Do what works for you!

PRACTICE:

Find a quiet, peaceful area (outside if possible) where you can practice your walking meditation. As you walk, notice the elements that occur in each step:

1. Lift one foot and move it forward while balancing on the other foot.
2. Starting with your heel, gently place your lifted foot on the ground in front of you.
3. Shift your weight onto your forward leg as the heel of your back foot lifts.
4. Synchronize your breathing with each movement (inhale as you lift, exhale as you step).

REFLECTION:

How does this practice make you mindful of your body?

How can you use this practice to meditate throughout your day?

What else does your body do for you when you're operating on autopilot?

DAY 8

REVAMP YOUR GROCERY LIST

PURPOSE:

Making healthy choices is far easier when you're well prepared. If you've got a fresh meal stored and ready for you in the fridge, you're less likely to be tempted by take-outs and drive-thrus. Your body (and wallet) will thank you.

PRACTICE:

Today's three-step practice takes some preparation, so don't worry if it extends into the next day or two.

1. Get out your favorite cookbook or foodie website and pick two healthy recipes for breakfast, lunch, and dinner (a few healthy snacks wouldn't hurt, either).
2. Make a list of all the ingredients you'll need for your healthy recipes.
3. Go shopping! Keep things simple and healthy by buying only what's on your list.

Heads up: Make space in your schedule tomorrow because you'll be preparing your meals!

REFLECTION:

Think of food as your fuel. How would this shift your mindset or change your relationship with your body?

How might this approach impact your diet?

How do you want to fuel yourself?

DAY 9

PREPARE HEALTHY MEALS

PURPOSE:

If you struggle to cook every single night of the week, remember that you don't have to! Today's meals can easily become tomorrow's leftovers so you can stay full and healthy (and resist the snack cupboard). Fill your body with the nutrients it needs by having meals prepared, stored, and waiting for you in the fridge or freezer.

PRACTICE:

Today builds on yesterday's practice of mindful planning. Prepare (cut, cook, and contain) your meals for the next few days using yesterday's recipes. Make things easy for yourself by preparing your meals in large portions and then dividing them into pre-portioned containers for each day.

MINDFUL TIP:

Set up a simple meal plan to stick on your fridge. This way, you can easily rotate meals throughout the week to keep things fresh.

REFLECTION:

How can meal prep benefit your diet and schedule?

How can you make this practice mindful and enjoyable?

How might it contribute to healthier living?

DAY 10

EAT WITHOUT DISTRACTION

PURPOSE:

When you eat, consider your distractions. Are you paying attention to what you're consuming and appreciating the time that went into making it? Can you identify the spices and flavors and how they blend together? Or are you checking your phone, watching TV, or tuning out from your day and yourself? Paying attention to what you eat fosters an attitude of gratitude and will help you to slow down and enjoy your food.

PRACTICE:

Just like you did in last week's breakfast exercise, remove distractions while you eat today. If you usually eat on the go, take time to sit down for your meals. Put away your phone, turn off the TV, and focus on the food you're consuming. Begin this exercise at breakfast and extend it into every meal. There will be no working through lunch today!

REFLECTION:

What usually distracts you while you're eating?

What did you experience (thoughts, feelings, challenges, flavors, etc.) when you ate your meals without distraction?

DAY 11

DO 20 MINUTES OF EXERCISE

PURPOSE:

Not only does regular exercise keep you physically fit, but it also greatly benefits your mental and emotional health by helping to relieve stress. Even 20 minutes a day can have a significant impact as you deepen your connection to yourself through movement and breath.

PRACTICE:

Commit at least 20 minutes today to your exercise of choice. Cycle to work or around the neighborhood, lift weights (or soup cans!), dance around your house, or follow along with an online yoga video. Do whatever makes you feel good!

REFLECTION:

What did you do for 20 minutes of exercise today?

How did you feel afterward?

What other exercises do you want to practice?

DAY 12

CREATE A HOME SPA

PURPOSE:

Many people get their best ideas in the shower because that's the only time and place they are truly alone and without distraction. How refreshed would you feel—both physically and mentally—if you extended your "shower mindfulness" for an hour or two?

PRACTICE:

Expand on the quiet, distraction-free benefits of the shower by designating 60 minutes to an at-home spa treatment. Prepare a hot bath, play relaxing music, and light a candle or diffuse essential oils. After you're done, wrap yourself in a cozy robe, make a cup of tea, read a book, write in your journal, or try out a guided meditation.

REFLECTION:

What did you do to relax?

What thoughts, feelings, and ideas came up during your hour of relaxation?

How did you feel afterward?

If applicable: What was challenging about dedicating 60 minutes to yourself?

DAY 13

BUILD A MORNING ROUTINE

PURPOSE:

Rather than giving in to the temptation of pressing snooze repeatedly, use a mindful morning routine to slowly ease into your day. While it may not sound as enticing as those few extra minutes of sleep, your morning routine will be much more valuable. Begin as you intend to continue: mindfully. Start with a mindful routine, and you will carry mindfulness with you throughout your day.

PRACTICE:

If you don't already have a morning routine, try these five simple steps:

1. When your alarm goes off the first time, sit up and turn on a light or quietly head into another room.
2. Take a deep breath, smile, and express gratitude for a new day.
3. Set an intention for the day ("Today, I will be, practice, or focus on _____").
4. Think of one thing you can do today to live out your intention and commit to doing it.
5. If you haven't already done so, now is the time to crawl out of bed. Move slowly, do some stretches, and make yourself a healthy breakfast.

REFLECTION:

What did your morning routine look like today?

How did it help you go about your day with intention and gratitude?

How do you want to begin your day tomorrow?

DAY 14

REFRESH YOURSELF

PURPOSE:

When your phone or computer is on the fritz, what's the first thing you do? Restart. When you feel frozen in the everyday roles and routines of life, take a moment to refresh. Unlike your computer, you don't have to shut down entirely, but you might have to devote time, space, and energy back into yourself and what matters to you.

PRACTICE:

Give yourself 15 minutes of attention when you need a quick refresher. Disconnect from daily distractions (I'm looking at you, email and social media). Go for a walk, listen to music, write in your journal, or sit quietly and focus on your breathing.

REFLECTION:

What pressures or distractions tend to drain your energy?

How do you know when you need to unplug?

What did you do today to refresh yourself?

DAY 15

DETOXIFY YOUR BODY

PURPOSE:

Unhealthy foods and harmful habits can decrease your energy, cause inflammation, and impact your mental health. Consuming foods that fuel you will build your awareness of and respect for your body and make you feel connected and comfortable within it.

PRACTICE:

Remove one unhealthy item or habit from your diet: caffeine, sugar, alcohol, or something else. If this is a monster task, start by avoiding it for today and replacing it with a healthy alternative (e.g., decaf or tea instead of coffee, natural honey instead of refined sugar).

MINDFUL TIP:

If possible, try this with a partner or friend. It's much easier (though still not easy!) to resist temptation when you have someone to hold you accountable. If this is an important practice for you, set a seven-, fourteen-, or thirty-day detox goal.

REFLECTION:

What food or habit did you choose to remove and why?

How did your body respond?

What did this practice reveal to you about how you want to treat your body?

DAY 16

GO THE EXTRA MILE

PURPOSE:

Getting out of your comfort zone can feel daunting or, at times, impossible. Starting with small choices can help you ease your way through discomfort and into growth. You might even find that the extra mile isn't as long as you thought!

PRACTICE:

Search for opportunities today that will push you slightly out of your comfort zone. Commit to doing one simple thing today, and then act on that choice. Take the stairs instead of the elevator, leave your phone behind while you run an errand, or get outside and run a mile. Remember that even small ripples can make waves.

REFLECTION:

How did you go the extra mile today?

How did you feel during this practice? Afterward?

What kind of ripples might this create?

DAY 17

TEND TO YOUR HEALTH

PURPOSE:

We often let our needs fall to the wayside while taking care of other people, priorities, and tasks. It's essential that you tend to your wellbeing for two main reasons:

1. You deserve your time and energy as much as anyone else does.
2. When you're healthy, you can better care for everyone and everything else.

PRACTICE:

Don't wait until illness or burnout before you start taking care of your health. Ask yourself (and answer honestly) if you would benefit from seeing a counselor, massage therapist, personal trainer, medical doctor, or naturopath. You might even consider dropping in on an exercise class or support group. If you believe one or more of these options would serve you well, book an appointment. Your future self will thank you.

REFLECTION:

Consider how your physical health impacts other aspects of your life, such as work, relationships, or running errands. Why is it important for you to take care of yourself?

How did you tend to your health today?

What signs does your body give to remind you to tend to your health?

DAY 18

DECLUTTER YOUR SPACE

PURPOSE:

If you're drowning in stuff that's "nice to have" or that you "might need someday," you may need to practice the art of letting go. Tidying your environment in your home, yard, office, or vehicle creates open, organized space around you, which can promote feelings of calmness and positivity.

PRACTICE:

Time for a little spring cleaning! (This may take a few days or weeks, and that's fine.)

1. Declutter. Sell or donate clothing and household items you don't regularly wear, use, or absolutely need.
2. Get organized. Once you've rid your space of unnecessary clutter, put everything that's left in its designated place.
3. Tidy up. Sweep, wash, vacuum, or do whatever you need to create a clean and cozy area you'll want to spend time in.
4. Observe. Spend time in your space and notice how it makes you feel.

MINDFUL TIP:

Remember to clean responsibly. Recycle, reuse, sell, trade, or donate your stuff. A local shelter or thrift shop is a far better option than the landfill.

REFLECTION:

How did this process change the way you look at what you own?

How did you define what was necessary versus unnecessary?

What did you learn about your relationship with the space around you?

CHAPTER ONE REFLECTION

Take a moment to reflect on the past 18 days and the commitment you have made to becoming aware of your physical self.

How have you learned to listen to and connect with your body?

Which practices resonated with you? Make a note of those you want to come back to.

Before moving forward:

- Be proud of the investment you've made in yourself.

- Recognize the insight you have gained because of the work you've done.

- Celebrate the growth you've experienced because you chose to grow.

- Remember your capacity for self-empowerment, fulfillment, and transformation.

- Believe that you will continue to connect to your inner wisdom should you choose to live with mindfulness.

CHAPTER TWO: EMOTIONAL

"We should examine ourselves and learn what is the affection and purpose of the heart, for in this way only can we learn what we honestly are."

—MARY BAKER EDDY

DAY 19

CHECK IN WITH YOURSELF

PURPOSE:

Checking in with yourself gives you insight into how you're doing, what you want or need, and what your next steps might be. Without regular self-assessment, you're likely to make decisions based on what others think or say you should do; by checking in, you gain self-awareness to make choices that align with your values.

PRACTICE:

List two to five questions you would like to ask each time you check in with yourself. Consider what you value or might want to keep track of as you assess different priorities in your life. If you're not sure where to begin, start with today's reflection questions.

REFLECTION:

How do you feel about your current lifestyle?

What are your deepest wants and needs right now?

Does your lifestyle meet these wants and needs?

How can you begin prioritizing what you value?

DAY 20

WRITE WHAT'S WRONG

PURPOSE:

It won't do you any good to keep issues and emotions bottled up inside because they will eventually come out one way or another. Getting things out of your head and onto paper allows you to identify your feelings and deal with what's causing them. This process will help you better handle your emotions so that you don't get overwhelmed or let unresolved issues turn into resentments and regrets.

PRACTICE:

Today is about addressing something that has hurt or bothered you. First, find a way to get it onto paper. Use the next page or a separate notebook if you want more room to write (or in case you want to rip up the pages after). Write, draw, or madly scribble about what's wrong. Identify what it is and why it upsets you. Get it all out on paper, then say it out loud or scream it into a pillow if you need to. Do what you need to get it out of your system!

If and when you feel a sense of release, take a few deep breaths and observe any feelings or sensations that arise.

MINDFUL TIP:

Visualize each emotion as a wave. Though it might feel like this wave has quickly and unbearably crashed upon you, know that this feeling will not last forever. No matter how uncomfortable or intense a feeling becomes, remember that this too shall pass.

REFLECTION:

How did this practice help you address an uncomfortable issue or emotion?

How did it help you to think of each emotion as a wave?

How can this process help you clarify, confront, or let go of emotional pain and overwhelm?

DAY 21

WRITE WHAT'S RIGHT

PURPOSE:

Celebrating yourself and being grateful for what you have can be a powerful tool for joy and abundance. When you compare your circumstances or yourself to others, you actively lessen your own joy and satisfaction. Instead, acknowledge your blessings and capabilities. This recognition empowers you and shifts your energy back to you so that you can continue doing the amazing things you're capable of.

PRACTICE:

Celebrate yourself! List three things under each reflection question and come back to your answers regularly. Smile and thank yourself once you've completed today's practice and each time you reflect upon it.

REFLECTION:

What are you grateful for?

1.

2.

3.

What do you love about yourself?

1.

2.

3.

What are you capable of?

1.

2.

3.

DAY 22

TELL SOMEONE WHAT'S WRONG

PURPOSE:

Whatever you're going through, know that you don't have to do it alone. Remember that you are a human being who lives in an interconnected system of people who are willing to support you. Even if someone else is unable to fully understand your struggle or story, it can make a world of difference to talk to someone and be heard.

PRACTICE:

Reach out to someone you trust, whether they're a partner, friend, family member, or counselor. Tell that person what you're dealing with and how they can support you.

MINDFUL TIP:

It can be hard to ask for help. Know that you are a human and not a burden. You deserve to feel vulnerable and supported as much as anyone else does.

REFLECTION:

Who do you turn to when you need support?

Who did you reach out to today?

How did it feel to be vulnerable with that person?

If applicable: Based on what you know of yourself (your history, tendencies, personal expectations, etc.), why might you find it challenging to be vulnerable with other people?

DAY 23

REFLECT ON HAPPY TIMES

PURPOSE:

Taking time to reflect on joyful memories reminds you of what you value and all that you have to celebrate. Not only is this practice fun, but it can also provide clarity when you're making important decisions, because it helps you focus your attention on what's meaningful to you. The Law of Attraction is the ability to attract into your life what you focus on. When you focus on joy and gratitude, you invite these into your life by consciously and subconsciously seeking them out.

PRACTICE:

Look at old photos, journals, or keepsakes from happy memories you have. Allow yourself to feel the emotions that arise as you reflect, and silently identify each one ("I feel _____ looking at this photo because _____"). Observe when, where, why, and with whom you experienced your happiest memories.

REFLECTION:

Which memories did you reflect on today?

What did this practice show you about what makes you happy and what you value?

What are some other happy memories you have?

DAY 24

FORGIVE SOMEONE

PURPOSE:

When you feel that someone has wronged you, it can be tempting to hold on to the sadness, resentment, or anger you feel toward them. But holding on to those feelings can end up hindering you through your thoughts, feelings, and relationships. Forgiving doesn't necessarily mean forgetting, but it does mean letting go of emotions that weigh you down; when you let them go, you can move forward.

PRACTICE:

If an individual or group has done something to upset you, start by doing your emotional work to deal with what happened. Write about it, talk to a friend, or seek professional counsel. If it's you that you need to forgive, admit wrongdoing and accept responsibility. Own it. And, just as you would expect from someone else, apologize to yourself. Write a letter or say your apology in the mirror. It may seem silly, but it's an important step in nurturing self-love and trust.

MORNING REFLECTION:

Are you harboring resentment or holding a grudge against someone?

How does this affect you?

How will forgiving that person change your life?

EVENING REFLECTION:

What was challenging about today's practice in forgiveness?

What emotions did you experience as you went through your process?

How did you feel afterward?

DAY 25

CELEBRATE YOUR GROWTH

PURPOSE:

When a negative thought or feeling sneaks up on you, it can be tough to shake. Taking time to focus on the positive things in your life helps balance your mind and gets you in the habit of celebrating where you are and how far you've come. This exercise is especially effective when you feel insecure or inadequate, as it brings your focus back to your blessings, strengths, and abilities.

PRACTICE:

Consider all you have to celebrate from this past week alone. What about this month or the whole year? Using the reflection questions, take time to recognize and record your blessings, accomplishments, and growth. Then make a plan to celebrate yourself!

REFLECTION:

Write down three things in your life worthy of celebration.

1.

2.

3.

What are three ways you've grown in the past year (big or small)?

1.

2.

3.

Choose one item from your list and write down the steps that went into your achievement or growth.

Now, how will you celebrate yourself?

DAY 26

JOURNAL ABOUT YOUR DREAMS

PURPOSE:

Reflecting on what you want is the first step toward making it happen. You can't just dream of it and wait for the universe to toss it down from the sky. Remember the Law of Attraction from your happy memory reflection a few days ago? You attract what you give your attention to. By identifying and focusing on your dreams and desires, you will invest more time and energy into making them happen.

PRACTICE:

When preparing to write about your dreams, think about your personal values (what's truly important to you) and lifestyle ideals (what you really want out of your big, beautiful life). Then dive into the following questions to explore your big-picture desires and determine how you can move closer toward them.

REFLECTION:

Values: When you look back on your life, how will you measure its importance?

Ideals: If money were no object, what would your dream life look like? What would you do if you knew you could not fail?

What is one thing you can do today to move closer to your dream life, even if it seems far away or impossible to reach?

DAY 27

WRITE YOURSELF A LETTER

PURPOSE:

Encouraging yourself will give you more confidence than any amount of likes or followers on social media. You manifest the messages you tell yourself (we'll dive into self-talk in the next chapter), so make sure to give yourself plenty of gentle love and support! Writing down your encouragement is a great way to believe in yourself in the moment and hold on to that message through future doubts. Plus, who doesn't love a good old handwritten letter?

PRACTICE:

Write yourself a letter (or multiple letters!) of support and set a date for when you will open it. If you have a six-month goal, you might write one letter to open in three months and another to open in six. Or maybe you write six short notes and open each one at the beginning of the month. Whatever your goal or timeline, write to yourself as if you were a dear friend in need of some kind words.

REFLECTION:

How did it feel to think of yourself as a friend?

How does this mindset reflect the way you treat yourself?

What messages do you need to tell yourself more often?

How might writing these messages to yourself help you build confidence and self-love?

DAY 28

TALK TO YOURSELF

PURPOSE:

Most of us are so used to (and good at) prioritizing others that we often forget to give ourselves the love and kindness we need. Remember that you deserve to experience the patience and appreciation you show to others. When you practice these things with yourself, they will not only fill you up, but also pour out of you and into your relationships.

PRACTICE:

Stand in front of a mirror and look yourself in the eye for 10 seconds. Tell yourself one specific thing you appreciate about yourself. Then, while maintaining eye contact, repeat the following:

> "I will be patient and kind with you."
> "I appreciate you just as you are."
> "I love you."

REFLECTION:

What did you tell yourself (or want to tell yourself)?

How did it feel to look yourself in the eye?

What did this practice reveal about the messages you usually tell yourself?

DAY 29

PRACTICE A MANTRA

PURPOSE:

Just as you walk where your feet are pointed, you move toward what your mind focuses on. Practicing a mantra (a repeated statement or affirmation) allows you to point your energy in the direction you want to go. Think of your mantra as a declaration of mindful commitment as you go about this practice of setting and stating your intention.

PRACTICE:

First, ask yourself what you want to see more of in your life. Then choose your mantra accordingly. You can use one of the examples below or write your own. Write your mantra on a piece of paper to carry in your pocket throughout the day.

"By cultivating happiness, I inspire others to be happy."
"I will practice joy in this moment."
"I am at peace with myself, just as I am."
"I love myself deeply and unconditionally."
"I believe in myself and what I am doing."
"Every day, I am becoming more successful."

REFLECTION:

What is your mantra for today?

Why is it important to you to focus on this?

What is one thing you can do today to turn your intention into reality?

DAY 30

EXPRESS YOURSELF

PURPOSE:

Self-expression is essential to awareness and love, especially since many of us spend so much time fitting into roles and boxes defined by others. Express yourself by doing something that makes you feel authentically you. You define yourself, and you do this by engaging in what makes you feel connected and fulfilled.

PRACTICE:

Spend 30 minutes on an activity that brings you closer to yourself by making you feel happy and in your element. Sing and dance to your favorite album, paint a picture, do yoga, or get your hands dirty in the garden. Whatever the activity, focus on what it feels like, rather than what it might look like (especially the dancing!). Have fun with being uniquely you.

REFLECTION:

What did you do during your 30 minutes of self-expression?

How did you feel during this time? After?

What other activities bring you joy through expression?

DAY 31

ENGAGE IN PLAY

PURPOSE:

Being creative means learning to do things differently—on your own terms. Unfortunately, this practice is often stifled by fear of judgment and making mistakes. Allowing yourself time to play, experiment, and laugh (yes, even at yourself) is a great way to overcome these fears, get out of your head, and have fun.

PRACTICE:

Make yourself laugh today. Practice ways to express yourself and goof around a little! Schedule at least 10 minutes of play, during which you do something simply for the sake of enjoyment. Even if it feels silly or uncomfortable, do it anyway. Life is too important to live without play!

REFLECTION:

How did you engage in play today?

What thoughts, feelings, or questions came up?

How did 10 minutes of being creative or goofy affect the rest of your day?

DAY 32

BE YOUR OWN DATE

PURPOSE:

Your relationship with yourself is the same as your relationship with other people: it requires that you spend time with you! In order to deepen your self-connection, you need to get to know who you are, what you like, and what's important to you. In order to know and love yourself, you must give yourself more time to reconnect!

PRACTICE:

Today you will take yourself out for a night (or day) on the town. Get ready as if you were meeting a friend or going on a date, and then spend an hour getting to know yourself. Try a yoga class, go for a hike, journal at a local coffee shop, or walk through the park or gallery. You might even make a list of questions you want to explore to get to know yourself better!

REFLECTION:

Write three sentences about what you did on your date and how you felt during and afterward.

1.

2.

3.

Do you believe that you deserve your love and attention just as much as anyone else does?

How do (or will) you act on this belief?

DAY 33

ACTIVELY LISTEN

PURPOSE:

Attention builds connection. Consider how it feels when you have someone's undivided attention: you feel heard, validated, and cared for. Look for opportunities to share that feeling (and your attention) with someone else through active, empathetic listening.

PRACTICE:

Seek out a face-to-face conversation. Make eye contact and pay attention to what the other person tells you. Rather than planning your response while they're talking, listen to the message they're sharing and what they might need from you. Be present in the interaction and value the connection (and *please* put your phone away!).

REFLECTION:

How do you feel when someone really listens to you?

What do you usually think about when listening to other people?

How did (and can) active listening transform your interactions?

DAY 34

ASSESS YOUR RELATIONSHIPS

PURPOSE:

Just as your life reflects what you spend most of your time and energy on, your beliefs and behaviors reflect those of the people you surround yourself with. You become like the company you keep. If you want to change your habits or thought patterns, consider who you spend time with.

PRACTICE:

Begin by finding a way to separate yourself from a person or situation that invites stress, negativity, or straight-up drama into your life. Relationships don't have to be as complicated as they often seem. Create space between you and those who cause emotional turmoil, and connect with someone who makes you feel calm, happy, and able to be yourself.

REFLECTION:

Identify any unhealthy relationships. What makes those relationships unhealthy?

How do you feel around that person (or those people)?

How does that relationship (or those relationships) negatively impact you?

Now, identify your healthy relationships. What makes those relationships healthy?

How do you feel around that person (or those people)?

Who would you like to spend more time with? And why?

DAY 35

IDENTIFY YOUR FEELINGS

PURPOSE:

How many feelings do you think you experience on an average day? You might find the number to be staggering. Thinking of your feelings as waves (as you practiced two weeks ago on day 20) can make difficult emotions easier to handle, as you know that each wave will break to make way for another. This practice is also a wonderful reminder to appreciate the joyful moments and to stay present while they occur.

PRACTICE:

Use this page or keep a small notebook with you to record your feelings today. As you go about your day, take note of the many emotions you experience; consider each one a wave that ebbs, flows, and breaks. As you identify and record each feeling, accept that it's happening, and acknowledge that it will eventually wash away.

REFLECTION:

What emotion do you feel right now?

Where did this feeling come from?

How do you usually respond when it feels like your emotions are taking over?

How did (or can) it help you to think of each emotion as a wave?

DAY 36

INVEST IN YOURSELF

PURPOSE:

What you do today is a direct investment in your life tomorrow. When making choices—whether big or small—consider how they will impact your future. What do you want your future to look like? And what can you do today, for *yourself*, to move closer to that vision?

PRACTICE:

Make a self-investment that leads you to action. Sign up for that fitness program, enroll in the course, or purchase those art supplies. Invest in what you value. This is how you get your biggest and most meaningful ROI (return on investment): personal satisfaction.

MINDFUL TIP:

Your financial investment is only one part of the equation. Your time is your most valuable resource—it is what your life is made of, after all—and you'll need to invest a whole lot of it into yourself in order to see your desired results!

REFLECTION:

What self-investment did you make today? Why?

What results do you want to see?

What will you need to do to create those results?

CHAPTER TWO REFLECTION

Take a moment to reflect on the past 18 days and the commitment you have made to becoming aware of your emotional self.

How have you learned to understand your feelings and better trust them?

Which practices resonated with you? Make a note of those you want to come back to.

Before moving forward:

- Be proud of the investment you've made in yourself.
- Recognize the insight you have gained because of the work you've done.
- Celebrate the growth you've experienced because you chose to grow.
- Remember your capacity for self-empowerment, fulfillment, and transformation.
- Believe that you will continue to connect to your inner wisdom should you choose to live with mindfulness.

CHAPTER THREE: RATIONAL

"All things are ready, if our mind be so."

—WILLIAM SHAKESPEARE

DAY 37

BEGIN UNPLUGGED

PURPOSE:

Taking time with and for yourself reconnects you to your wants, needs, and goals. This is especially important first thing in the morning, as this is when you set the tone for your entire day. Avoiding email, social media, and other digital distractions gives you the space to add more focus and awareness to your morning so you can build habits for a meaningful day.

PRACTICE:

Begin your day without distraction by practicing a short morning routine that's simple and centered on you. Flip back to day 13 to review the morning routine you practiced in Chapter One. Or, simply take five deep breaths, stretch for five minutes, then make and eat breakfast sitting down at the table without technology or distractions.

REFLECTION:

What was your unplugged morning routine?

How did it allow you to connect to yourself and the present moment?

How did your routine impact your mindset throughout the day?

DAY 38

START WITH WHAT'S IMPORTANT

PURPOSE:

Urgent demands can pop up left, right, and center, and usually at the most inconvenient times. Ensure that you do what's most important to you before you get hit with someone else's curveball. Doing what's important to you early in the day will spare you the frustration of trying to cram it in last thing before bed (or skip it entirely).

PRACTICE:

What is the most important thing you want or need to do for yourself today? Commit to this by doing it before work or setting a midday reminder to make sure you focus your energy on your biggest priority! Set a specific amount of time aside so you can do what's important with intention and without distraction.

REFLECTION:

What is the most important thing for you to do today?

How did you do this with intention?

How much time will you set aside each day to continue doing what's important to you?

When will you do this?

DAY 39

SAY "THANK YOU"

PURPOSE:

Your language both reflects and impacts the way you think and behave. Though saying "please" and "thank you" may seem trivial, it's a powerful practice. Politeness can go a long way in benefiting your interactions and building a mindset of gratitude.

PRACTICE:

Make it your mission to fit "please" and "thank you" into every conversation you have today. If you're already a master of manners, focus on replacing "sorry" with "thank you." For example, "Sorry I'm late" could turn into "Thank you for being patient." Or instead of saying, "I'm sorry I was in a bad mood," you might try, "Thank you for listening and lifting my spirits."

REFLECTION:

What did this exercise reveal to you about your language?

How did changing your language impact your interactions?

How did it help you cultivate a mindset of appreciation and positivity?

DAY 40

OBSERVE YOUR SELF-TALK

PURPOSE:

Your self-talk is the dialogue that runs through your head during every moment of every day. The messages you repeatedly tell yourself become the narrative you believe about who you are, what you can do, and what you deserve. These narratives impact (or can entirely determine) your self-esteem, performance, and relationships.

PRACTICE:

Pay attention today to how you speak to yourself. As you go about your day, identify and challenge the unhealthy messages you tell yourself. Say "no" aloud or in your head when you call yourself a name, compare yourself to others, complain about something, or tell yourself you "should" be a different way.

MINDFUL TIP:

Pair this exercise with that of day 29 and practice a mantra of positive self-talk. When you catch yourself saying "no" to a negative message, replace it with one of love and acceptance.

REFLECTION:

What did you notice about your self-talk?

How does your self-talk affect your self-esteem and relationships?

What loving, empowering messages do you want to tell yourself more often?

DAY 41

WRITE YOUR PRIORITIES

PURPOSE:

Pay attention to what you want, and you will invest more time and energy into it. As you know from the previous mention of the Law of Attraction, clearly identifying what you value and desire is essential to living your ideals. Writing down what matters to you is a great first step, as it gives you clarity, keeps you accountable, and allows you to reflect on your progress.

PRACTICE:

Today is all about exploring what deeply matters to you. Dig into today's questions to explore your personal priorities and plan how to pursue them. Resist the temptation to edit your thoughts and ideas as you answer each question. Simply write the first few things that come to mind and see where it takes you!

REFLECTION:

What is important to you?

What does a meaningful day look like to you?

How do you want to be as a person? Which attributes do you want to adopt or improve?

Review your answers. Why have you chosen these values and priorities?

DAY 42

THEME YOUR DAYS

PURPOSE:

Theming is the practice of directing your focus with scheduled intentions. If something doesn't make it onto your schedule, chances are slim that it will get done. By assigning a theme or intention to each day, you commit to investing your time and energy into that intention. This ensures that you do what's important and grow in ways that are meaningful to you.

PRACTICE:

Using your answers from yesterday's exercise, organize your list of personal priorities into categories (or themes). Publishing a book, for instance, could fit into a Writing or Business Development category. Spending time with your partner or children could fall under Family. Stick to categories that reflect important goals (what you want to do) and values (how you want to live).

Once your list is relatively organized, assign one category to each day of the week. Maybe Sunday is for Family, Monday for Writing, Tuesday for Creativity, etc. Don't be afraid to experiment to find what works best with your schedule.

MINDFUL TIP:

Remember that your theme will not be the only thing you do that day. The idea is simply that it will give you a clearer picture of how to plan your day and where to focus your thoughts.

REFLECTION:

List your daily themes and how you plan to act on each one:

Monday:

Tuesday:

Wednesday:

Thursday:

Friday:

Saturday:

Sunday:

How will this added focus help you make time for what's important to you?

DAY 43

EXERCISE A STRENGTH

PURPOSE:

Knowing what you're good at is one thing; practicing it is another. Exercising one of your strengths can empower you to build your skills or try something completely new. More importantly, it boosts your confidence and helps you recognize the gift you are!

PRACTICE:

Own your strengths. Whether it's a sport, an art, or your ability to communicate well with others, start by identifying what you're good at. Feel free to ask others for insight, but do your best to answer this for yourself first. Then choose one strength and find a way to practice it today.

REFLECTION:

List your strengths and abilities below.

Which strength did you exercise today?

How did you feel about yourself afterward?

DAY 44

TRY SOMETHING NEW

PURPOSE:

If you struggle to try new things, it may be due to a perfectionist mindset, which leads to frustration or defeat when you don't pick up new skills right away. Practice embracing life's learning curves with an open mind and a good sense of humor so you can appreciate the process of learning—even when it's slow or uncomfortable.

PRACTICE:

Choose one thing you've always wanted to learn but simply haven't given yourself the time or patience to try. Hop on those skis, talk to that person, draw that picture. Today is your day to give it a shot and have fun with it!

MINDFUL TIP:

This practice is one of curious exploration. Try not to take your activity (or yourself) too seriously!

REFLECTION:

What new thing did you try today?

How did it feel to be a beginner?

What did your self-talk sound like during this process?

DAY 45

VALUE YOUR GROWTH

PURPOSE:

It's important to step out of the constant flow of everyday life to evaluate your decisions, celebrate your growth, and seek out new opportunities. Thinking and writing about how an experience has shaped your life can help you to see its value while encouraging you to be open to new experiences.

PRACTICE:

Reflect on how you've grown from the last two practices, in which you exercised a strength and tried something new. Then answer today's reflection questions.

Heads up: Once you've completed your reflection, read ahead to tomorrow's exercise, as it requires a bit of planning.

REFLECTION:

What did you gain by exercising a strength?

How did this impact your mindset when trying something new?

What was challenging about trying something new?

What was rewarding?

How did you grow from this experience?

DAY 46

DETOXIFY YOUR MIND

PURPOSE:

There are a number of exercises in this book that invite you to remove physical and mental clutter. This is because distraction-free moments are what lead to deep awareness and self-connection. While a digital detox may be a challenging practice, consider all that you can gain from stepping away from habitual distractions.

PRACTICE:

Detoxify your mind by disconnecting from social media, television, online games, and other forms of digital entertainment. Instead, use today to do one of four things:

1. Connect with yourself.
2. Connect with others in person.
3. Practice a skill or learn a new one.
4. Choose a previous activity from this book to practice again.

REFLECTION:

What was most challenging about this exercise?

What did it show you about your media habits?

Which of the four options did you focus on today?

How did that benefit you?

DAY 47

ATTEND TO AUTOPILOT

PURPOSE:

Like most people, you probably spend a lot of time doing things on autopilot: washing the dishes, commuting to work, cleaning, running errands, and so on. But there is much to be gained by being present (i.e., paying attention) during your everyday tasks and routines. Everything you do can be an opportunity to cultivate mindfulness and gratitude.

PRACTICE:

Choose one thing you usually do on autopilot and pay close attention to that activity. Listen to a podcast on your way to work or drive in silence to practice positive self-talk. As you clean the house, practice your walking meditation from the beginning of this book (day 7). While cooking, eating, and washing dishes, silently express your gratitude for good food and clean water. Whatever the task, ask yourself how you can be present and grateful for it.

REFLECTION:

Which autopilot activity did you pay attention to?

How did paying attention change the way you performed this task?

How will you continue this practice to add mindfulness to everyday tasks?

DAY 48

REFLECT ON TODAY

PURPOSE:

You know by now that reflection is key to acknowledging personal progress, identifying opportunities for growth, and figuring out how to best move forward. Effective, long-lasting growth occurs through intention, and you can add a great deal of intention to your life through a practice of regular reflection.

PRACTICE:

In the morning, read over today's reflection questions and think about how you'd like to answer them at the end of the day. Then, before bed, answer each question honestly to reflect on today and to approach the days ahead with added intention.

REFLECTION:

Did you have a good day today? Why or why not?

What were you mindful of today?

What's one thing you did to really make today matter? (This is a great question to steer the days ahead in a meaningful direction!)

DAY 49

PREPARE FOR TOMORROW

PURPOSE:

Moving in the right direction is only possible when you know where you want to go. Instead of spending your day in "catch-up" mode from the night before, use your evening to prepare for tomorrow. Think of this preparation as your foundation or springboard for the next day so you can dive in with clarity and confidence.

PRACTICE:

Create and practice a simple evening routine to help you wind down from today and prepare for tomorrow. Set a certain time this evening (and, ideally, each evening) to disconnect from technology. Tidy your space, prepare your lunch, and pick out tomorrow's clothes. Then have a cup of tea, spend time with your loved ones, or read that book that's been sitting on your nightstand for the last month (we both know it's not there for décor)!

REFLECTION:

What was your evening routine?

How did it help you wind down from today?

How will it benefit you tomorrow?

DAY 50

CONSUME CONSCIOUSLY

PURPOSE:

Minimalism has taken off like wildfire in the Western world as people realize that life is so much more than stuff (and that too much stuff can get in the way of life). This mindset challenges our superficial attachment to material items and encourages practices like decluttering your space, recycling or donating what you don't need, and consuming (purchasing) responsibly. As a consumer, your spending habits can support certain people, groups, and ideas, and contribute to the way society functions.

PRACTICE:

Ask yourself how you can consume more responsibly. Pick one of these ideas to act on today:

- Purchase locally grown food.
- Buy second-hand clothing or arrange a clothing swap with friends.
- Use reusable bags at the grocery store.
- Bring your own travel mug to the coffee shop.
- Buy in bulk when possible to reduce plastic.
- Reuse sandwich bags or switch to containers.
- Learn more about recycling and composting.

MINDFUL TIP:

Make it fun! Create a game to encourage your children to recycle. Arrange a clothing drive and donate your goods to a shelter or thrift store. Get your friends involved so you can keep track of your progress and keep each other accountable.

REFLECTION:

What did you do today to be a more conscious consumer?

What wasteful habits do you need to challenge or break?

Does too much "stuff" ever get in the way of your life? If so, how?

DAY 51

MEDITATE IN SMALL DOSES

PURPOSE:

Creating and enjoying moments throughout the day when you can just be present in the here and now is crucial. When you focus too much on being someone or somewhere else, you distract yourself by trying to live in the future. Don't forget that you are a miraculous human being, walking the face of a planet floating through the cosmos. Your existence is amazing. Now it's time to act like it!

PRACTICE:

Practice a mini-meditation three times today: once in the morning, again in the afternoon, and one more time in the evening. To help you do this, set three alarms—one at each meal, if that's easiest—to act as reminders. At each alarm, do this three-minute awareness exercise:

- During minute 1, focus on the breath, practicing your deep breathing exercise from day 1.

- During minute 2, focus on the body, doing the massage or relaxation practice from day 5.

- During minute 3, focus on the mind; close your eyes, sit still, and observe your thoughts and feelings.

MINDFUL TIP:

During the last minute, acknowledge your thoughts or feelings as they come and go. Imagine placing each one on a leaf and setting it afloat on the surface of a slow-moving river that gently carries it away. Rather than judging your thoughts or striving for an empty mind, simply notice what comes up; then thank your brain for bringing this to your attention and send the thought on its way.

REFLECTION:

How did these mini-meditations add mindfulness to your day?

What did you notice during this practice?

How might regularly connecting to your breath, body, and mind benefit your life?

DAY 52

ASSESS YOUR WORRIES

PURPOSE:

The more time and energy you devote to a worry, the more emphasis your brain places on it. However, if you practice responding to your worries objectively, you will see that they are either giving you an opportunity to solve a problem that's within your control, or to let go of something outside of your control. Getting your worries down on paper helps you see things clearly so you can get to the root of the issue and find a solution, or simply move on.

PRACTICE:

Write three things that have you feeling worried or panicked today. For each worry, consider the reflection questions for today.

MINDFUL TIP:

Remember that by ruminating on a small worry, you can conjure up feelings of intense fear and uncertainty. This isn't because your worry is worth these feelings, but because you are telling your brain to perceive this worry as an immediate threat. Your brain then evokes fear or panic to ensure that you respond and protect yourself. This is what gives your small worry a big shadow.

REFLECTION:

What are you worried about and why?

Is this going to matter next week? Next year?

Is the outcome of this worry within your control?

If so, what can you do about it?

If not, how can you move past it or let it go?

DAY 53

ADDRESS YOUR WORRIES

PURPOSE:

If something is beyond your ability to control, it won't do you any good to worry. And even if you can do something, worrying still won't serve you because worrying doesn't create change. Worrying doesn't actually achieve anything aside from stressing you out! On the other hand, taking action will yield solutions, so focus your attention on what is within your control.

PRACTICE:

Reflect on the last two questions from yesterday's exercise, where you identified whether or not each worry is within your control. For the worries you can do something about, take one small, actionable step. For those outside of your control, do what you can to challenge your worried thoughts and start moving past them.

MINDFUL TIP:

Remind yourself that even if you can't change an event or its outcome, you are still in control of your actions and reactions.

REFLECTION:

How did you act on the worries you can control and change?

How did you change the way you approach those worries outside of your control?

What did you learn about your worries and the concept of worry in general?

DAY 54

CELEBRATE CHANGE

PURPOSE:

Without reflection, you might not recognize the changes you experience as you shift and grow throughout your life. Since you're now halfway through this book, take a moment to reflect on your progress and celebrate yourself. Remember that you've experienced meaningful, personal growth because you made the decision to grow. You've made purposeful strides that will benefit your mindset, environment, relationships, and more. Now's your time to acknowledge how far you've come and to become even more excited for what's ahead.

PRACTICE:

While answering today's reflection questions, consider the strengths and abilities you've practiced in the past 54 days. Then pour yourself a celebratory beverage and do a little happy dance! You deserve a day of recognition.

REFLECTION:

What have you learned about yourself in the last two months?

Which practices have you found most valuable so far?

How have they benefited you?

What changes have you made or experienced in your body, emotions, and mindset?

CHAPTER THREE REFLECTION

Take a moment to reflect on the past 18 days and the commitment you have made to becoming aware of your rational self.

How have you learned to observe your thought patterns to gain mental clarity?

Which practices resonated with you? Make a note of those you want to come back to.

Before moving forward:

- Be proud of the investment you've made in yourself.
- Recognize the insight you have gained because of the work you've done.
- Celebrate the growth you've experienced because you chose to grow.
- Remember your capacity for self-empowerment, fulfillment, and transformation.
- Believe that you will continue to connect to your inner wisdom should you choose to live with mindfulness.

CHAPTER FOUR: SPIRITUAL

"The foundations of a person are not in matter but in spirit."

—RALPH WALDO EMERSON

DAY 55

DEFINE YOUR SPIRITUALITY

PURPOSE:

The first step toward finding what you seek is *knowing* what you seek. Defining what spirituality means or looks like to you—whether it's a higher power, collective consciousness, personal purpose, or something else—can provide guidance as you search for meaning and connection.

PRACTICE:

Write down your definition of spirituality and any questions you have surrounding your beliefs.

MINDFUL TIP:

Take the pressure off by remembering that your definition doesn't have to completely encapsulate your whole belief system from now until the end of time. Beliefs and interpretations can shift and change as you move through life; consider what resonates with you at *this* point in your life.

REFLECTION:

What is your current definition of spirituality?

How does this definition reflect your values or what you want in life?

Based on your definition, what are some things you can do to grow spiritually?

DAY 56

PRACTICE YOUR SPIRITUALITY

PURPOSE:

Now that you've gained clarity by defining your spirituality, you can develop a practice to gain a deeper sense of purpose and understanding. Yesterday, you asked yourself what you can do to grow spiritually. Devote time to those practices so you can deepen your relationship with your beliefs and act on your values.

PRACTICE:

Reflect on the list of spiritual practices you wrote down yesterday. Today—right now—choose one practice and spend at least 10 minutes giving it your full attention. Depending on your definition of spirituality, you may choose to spend time in guided meditation, prayer, or study. You might also journal, paint, walk through nature, or help someone in need.

REFLECTION:

What did you do today to practice your spirituality?

How did this activity reflect your definition of spirituality?

How did you feel during and after this practice?

DAY 57

CULTIVATE GRATITUDE

PURPOSE:

Gratitude is a wonderful catalyst for happiness and fulfillment. By acknowledging and appreciating all the good things you have and have done, you empower yourself to recognize the benefits you deserve and the good things you are capable of. Practicing gratitude brings your focus to the present moment and reminds you that your fulfillment is not a hidden treasure for you to find, but a practice that requires regular attention and intention.

PRACTICE:

Write down what you are thankful for. Keep writing until you've filled the space below or a full page of your journal. Review your list and consider how each item contributes to your personal fulfillment. Then close your eyes, take a deep breath, and practice a mantra of gratitude (a quick "thank you" will do the trick).

REFLECTION:

How did you feel after this exercise?

How can cultivating gratitude bring you happiness and fulfillment?

What is your definition of fulfillment?

DAY 58

CREATE A SACRED SPACE

PURPOSE:

Consider where you spend the majority of your time. What does this space look or feel like? The calm or chaos of your environment impacts you in extraordinary ways. Creating a sacred space can do wonders for your mood, mindset, and habits—both while you're in the space and once you leave.

PRACTICE:

Tidy up your home, office, studio, or wherever you spend a significant amount of time. Organize what's essential and get rid of whatever causes distraction or creates clutter. Then consider adding one thing that gives your space a sense of calm, like a plant, candle, photo, or piece of artwork. Do something to make your space feel cozy, safe, and inviting.

REFLECTION:

What does your sacred space look and feel like?

How does it impact you?

What does this tell you about your relationship with the space around you?

DAY 59

MEET LIKE-MINDED PEOPLE

PURPOSE:

The company you keep will influence where you go and how you get there. Make sure you're moving forward with those who love and care for you and who will steer you in a positive direction. These are the ones who will keep you accountable and support you to go farther than you would ever imagine on your own.

PRACTICE:

Think of one like-minded person who will love and support you in a way you find meaningful. Once you can identify this individual and your shared values or interests, reach out and arrange a conversation, or schedule a time to get together. Avoid the urge to set an agenda for your time together and simply focus on building or deepening your connection with this lovely individual.

REFLECTION:

What kind of person or people do you want to connect with?

Who did you reach out to today?

How does (or might) their presence enrich your life?

DAY 60

PLAN A SACRED DAY

PURPOSE:

Think back to day 46, when you bravely worked to detoxify your mind from media. Similarly, the purpose of a sacred day is to set aside one day of the week to focus on deepening your awareness of and connection to your spirituality and self.

PRACTICE:

Intend on making today a sacred day to focus on your purpose, spiritual questions, or self-connection. Take time to connect with good friends, relax your mind and body, practice worship or meditation, or reflect on your personal purpose and priorities. Do what you can to insert your version of sacred thoughts and activities into your day.

MINDFUL TIP:

Revisit your daily themes from day 42. If you feel it would benefit you to do today's practice regularly, assign one of your days to sacredness or self-nourishment.

REFLECTION:

What does a sacred day look like to you?

What did you focus on to make today sacred?

How will you use future sacred days to nourish your spirit, soul, or self-awareness?

DAY 61

CONNECT TO YOUR BREATH

PURPOSE:

You are a collection of many interconnected elements, a circle of life. Tuning in to these elements, like your breath, brings balance to your body and lifestyle and allows you to build a deeper connection to what makes you truly *you*.

PRACTICE:

Today's connecting practice involves three distinct rounds of deep breathing, each consisting of 10 breaths.

1. DEEP BREATHS (X 10)

Begin by sitting tall in a chair, planting your feet on the ground, and placing your hands on your abdomen. For your first round, pay close attention to the way your body moves. As you inhale, feel your abdomen rise and expand as it fills with air. As you exhale, feel it contract and release.

2. GRATITUDE MANTRA (X 10)

Next, try this practice in a different position: standing, laying on your back, or seated against a wall with your legs stretched out in front of you. Cultivate gratitude with each breath by repeating a mantra in your head:

> (Inhale) "As I inhale, I receive energy."
> (Exhale) "As I exhale, I give joy."

> (Inhale) "I give thanks for this breath."
> (Exhale) "I am alive in this moment."

3. VISUALIZATION AND MOVEMENT (X 10)

As you inhale, imagine new energy pouring into your body and spirit like a bright light. Take up as much space as possible as you breathe in, pulling back your shoulders and reaching out your arms to invite in new, positive energy.

On your exhale, release the breath out of your mouth and let your body relax (like you're deflating). As you do this, visualize your mind releasing negative thoughts and your spirit letting go of negative energy.

REFLECTION:

What did you experience while doing each breathing exercise?

How did you connect to your body, mind, and spirit?

How might a simple breathing exercise become a spiritual practice?

Use this page to draw anything that reflects how you felt before and after this practice.

DAY 62

ASK YOURSELF QUESTIONS

PURPOSE:

Inquiry fosters self-awareness, which allows you to identify and understand your values and purpose with greater clarity. Think of your relationship with yourself like you would any other friendship you have. What do you know about yourself? What do you keep hidden?

PRACTICE:

Write down everything you know about yourself until you've filled the space on this (or a separate) page. Use the reflection questions or explore your own, and remember to encourage yourself with positive self-talk through this process!

REFLECTION:

What do you like to spend time doing?

When do you feel most yourself?

What are your strengths?

What have you achieved or overcome?

What makes you uncomfortable, frustrated, and angry?

What do you value?

What are your deepest dreams and desires?

Why are these things important to you?

What are some questions you still have for yourself?

DAY 63

MEDITATE ON BEAUTY

PURPOSE:

Seeking and appreciating the beauty around you is a powerful and refreshing practice for your mind and spirit. Meditation, like mindfulness, is about paying attention. Meditating on something you find beautiful or peaceful deepens your appreciation for these things and trains your brain to recognize beauty and peace in your life.

PRACTICE:

Find something beautiful and focus your attention on it (but try not to stare at strangers!). Light a candle and spend a few minutes watching it flicker and dance. Go for a walk and observe the life that surrounds you: trees, flowers, birds, clouds, or people. Or practice yoga, noticing your breath and the way your body moves and flows. Choose anything you find beautiful or peaceful and bask in the wonder of it.

REFLECTION:

How did you meditate on beauty today?

What did you feel and experience during this practice?

How did it impact your relationship with what you observed?

DAY 64

CREATE YOUR MANTRA

PURPOSE:

A mantra is a repeated affirmation or statement of intention. The repetition of it keeps your intention at the forefront of your mind, informing your brain of its significance and reminding you to seek out opportunities to fulfill it. Creating your own mantra requires you to look within and ask yourself questions to determine the message that matters to you.

PRACTICE:

Consider what you want to focus on today and set that as your intention. Then structure your intention into a simple statement that's meaningful to you. For instance, if you want to nurture a certain attribute, you could simply say, "Today, I will practice ___." If you need a day of encouragement or self-love, you might choose a positive affirmation: "I am ___" or "I deserve ___." Stick to a simple statement that you'll remember to tell yourself throughout the day.

MINDFUL TIP:

Write your mantra on a piece of paper and keep it in your pocket. Set hourly alarms throughout your day to remind yourself to read it. Say your mantra out loud every time you read it, so you are literally and continuously giving yourself loving, empowering messages.

REFLECTION:

What was your mantra for today?

Why is this something you want to nurture or practice?

How did telling yourself this message impact you?

What can you do to turn this mantra into action?

DAY 65

LISTEN TO THE MUSIC

PURPOSE:

Music has the ability to quickly and profoundly affect your mood, perceptions, and more. One song (or one line of a song) can make you feel understood and inspired or incredibly heartbroken in a matter of minutes. Similar to self-talk, listening to music with positive or meaningful lyrics helps you incorporate those messages into your life.

PRACTICE:

Find a meaningful song that you enjoy and listen to it in a quiet place free from distraction. Close your eyes and pay close attention to the message in the song, observing how it makes you feel.

REFLECTION:

What song did you listen to?

Why does this song resonate with you?

How did you feel while listening to it?

How can you apply its message to your life?

DAY 66

FIND SILENCE

PURPOSE:

Separating yourself from the noise and routine of everyday life can seem like an impossible task, but it is certainly worth the effort. Immersing yourself in an environment where you can experience quiet and solitude is a sure-fire way to find connection. Doing so in a natural setting can help you feel calm and grounded as you reconnect with your environment and yourself.

PRACTICE:

Seek out a quiet, natural environment for today's practice. Spend time in a local park, a nearby forest, at the edge of the ocean or a river or lake, or even your own backyard. Sit on a bench, lie under a tree, or walk barefoot through the grass. Practice being still and silent for a few minutes, breathing deeply and observing your surroundings.

MINDFUL TIP:

Repeat one of the breathing or meditation exercises you did earlier this week (days 61 and 63 respectively) to help you focus on your breath and the beauty around you.

REFLECTION:

Where did you go to find silence?

How did you feel in this environment?

How did it help you find connection?

How can you create more stillness and silence in your life?

DAY 67

NOURISH YOUR SOUL

PURPOSE:

There are many things you do out of obligation or because of your roles and responsibilities for others. It's important to balance these obligations with practices for yourself in order to maintain your identity and energy—not only for your own sake, but also for the good of others.

PRACTICE:

Find an activity that brings you joy or makes you feel like *you*. If there's something you love to do but never seem to find the time for it, make time today! Soul-nourishing activities can include writing, listening to music, creating art, singing and dancing, tending to your garden, building something, trying a new recipe, or working on a dream project. Alternatively, you might find nourishment by sitting in stillness and doing nothing at all.

REFLECTION:

What did you do to nourish your soul today?

How did you feel during this activity?

What other activity might nourish your soul?

DAY 68

WATCH THE SUN RISE OR SET

PURPOSE:

Watching the sun rise and set is a simple practice that can feel *so* magical. Not only can you observe the opening and closing of the day, but you also get a front-row seat to a live art show in the sky. Use this beautiful opportunity to begin and/or end your day with gratitude for the possibilities, lessons, and wonder that one day can hold.

PRACTICE:

Depending on your schedule, make it a point to watch today's sunrise or sunset. Bring this book (or your journal) with you and make an event of it. Take time to reflect on your spiritual definition, ask yourself questions, or practice gratitude. Or simply sit in silence, appreciating how the light transforms the sky while remembering that you are part of a magnificent world and infinite universe.

REFLECTION:

The sun rises and sets every single day; what made today special?

What did you observe, ask, or reflect on?

How was this a spiritual practice?

DAY 69

SEARCH FOR BEAUTY

PURPOSE:

You will find beauty in the world if you know how to recognize and pay close attention to it. This seek-and-you-shall-find approach presents itself through our ongoing discussion about the Law of Attraction and in this book's opening paragraph about awakening to your inner wisdom and potential. Once you define beauty by the way something makes you feel rather than what it looks like, you will become aware of the true beauty in your surroundings and yourself.

PRACTICE:

Seek out three beautiful things today (visuals, sensations, experiences, etc.) and keep track of what you find. This could be a flower or friendship, an image or interaction, a mountain or moment, or whatever else strikes you as beautiful. Take a photo or video or write a descriptive summary to record each finding, doing your best to capture why you found it beautiful.

REFLECTION:

What were your three findings?

1.

2.

3.

What made each one beautiful?

1.

2.

3.

What did your search show you about how you define beauty?

DAY 70

SHARE YOUR FINDINGS

PURPOSE:

Storytelling plays a major role in the way you build connections. Sharing and hearing about meaningful experiences allows you to communicate your values, teach important lessons, and practice gratitude and mindful reflection. By sharing something positive with others, you may even encourage them to seek the good in their lives and themselves.

PRACTICE:

Share a story or observation from yesterday's practice with someone you know. Reflect on what you found, what made it beautiful, and how your search for beauty impacted you.

MINDFUL TIP:

Share your story on social media so we can inspire and learn from one another!

REFLECTION:

How did sharing your story deepen your experience?

How can storytelling help you build meaningful connections?

What other experiences do you want to share with others?

DAY 71

ASK BIG QUESTIONS

PURPOSE:

Awareness comes through inquiry and introspection. As much as we might like to believe that life's answers will eventually float down from the sky, in reality, important answers generally arise from asking and wrestling with tough questions. Even if you can never be certain about some of those answers (I'm looking at you, existential questions!), exploring your questions will make you more aware of what's important to you and why.

PRACTICE:

Write down some of the big questions you have about your life and yourself, no matter how far-fetched or abstract they may seem. Feel free to explore one or more of the reflection questions if any of them resonate with your search.

REFLECTION:

Write down your big questions on the previous page or choose from the following:

- *What do you think your purpose is? How did you come to this answer?*
- *How can you fulfill your purpose or live a fulfilled life?*
- *Who are you? How do you identify yourself?*
- *What does it mean to be present?*
- *When you're at the end of your life, what will you want to look back on?*

Why is it important to you to ask (and potentially answer) this question?

Do you think the answer is out there for you to discover, or is it something you must create for yourself?

DAY 72

EXPLORE THE MYSTERY

PURPOSE:

A favorite mantra of mine is, "The progress is in the process." When you're exploring your big questions, the goal or measure of success is not necessarily the presence of an immediate answer (or any answer, for that matter). Focus instead on learning about yourself, becoming more comfortable with deep introspection, and cultivating an appreciation for the mystery.

PRACTICE:

Choose one question from yesterday's list and find a way to explore it. If you're one to write things down, use this page (or your journal) to keep track of thoughts and ideas that come to mind. Alternatively, you could record a voice memo or video in which you ask your question and address the thoughts that arise. Choose whatever medium you prefer and make it yours!

MINDFUL TIP:

Give yourself time to explore your big question on your own. Discovering the answer is only one part of the equation; remember that this is your process of introspection and interpretation—and your progress is in your process.

REFLECTION:

What was your process for exploring your personal or existential question?

How did shifting your focus from answering to exploring help you approach your question?

How might this help you approach other big questions you have?

How can you practice appreciating the mysteries of life without a need for answers?

CHAPTER FOUR REFLECTION

Take a moment to reflect on the past 18 days and the commitment you have made to becoming aware of your spiritual self.

How have you learned to explore your relationship with yourself and your truth?

Which practices resonated with you? Make a note of those you want to come back to.

Before moving forward:

- Be proud of the investment you've made in yourself.
- Recognize the insight you have gained because of the work you've done.
- Celebrate the growth you've experienced because you chose to grow.
- Remember your capacity for self-empowerment, fulfillment, and transformation.
- Believe that you will continue to connect to your inner wisdom should you choose to live with mindfulness.

CHAPTER FIVE: OCCUPATION

"It's not enough to be busy; so are the ants. The question is, what are we busy about?"

—HENRY DAVID THOREAU

DAY 73

ASSESS YOUR WORK

PURPOSE:

Think of an assessment as a strategic reflection. Your strategy is to first understand what you're doing and how it's working; then, you can determine what changes you should make to be more effective, productive, and fulfilled. Like reflection, assessment helps you identify your progress and point yourself toward your definition of success.

PRACTICE:

Start by choosing your area of assessment and make a list of the questions you have. You might consider reviewing your tools, strategies, progression, or personal satisfaction. Next, use your questions or today's reflection questions to honestly look at what's working and what changes you might need to make.

REFLECTION:

Which areas of your work are most important for you to assess? Why?

Rate your productivity at work. What makes you more or less efficient?

In what ways does your current work situation meet your needs and personal priorities?

In which areas are you stagnant or unsatisfied? Why?

What results do you seek? What changes will you make to achieve these results?

DAY 74

CELEBRATE YOUR SUCCESSES

PURPOSE:

Identifying and celebrating your successes can provide you with a newfound confidence to complete a project or take on something new. In the long run, this practice reveals what's worked for you in the past so you can apply those successful approaches to your current and future endeavors.

PRACTICE:

Make a list of your professional accomplishments, from little victories to iconic promotions. Whether you deem it to be a small win or a massive success, document each achievement. Next, arrange your list chronologically. Celebrate the steps you've taken and the growth you've created for yourself.

REFLECTION:

How do you feel about your professional accomplishments?

Which successes are you most proud of?

How do you define "success?"

DAY 75

WRITE YOUR GOALS

PURPOSE:

When you identify specific goals for your work—whether around a client, project, or your job in general—you give yourself (and others) direction. You create a purposeful strategy, which guides you toward your target with clarity and focus. You set yourself up for success.

PRACTICE:

First, focus on either one specific project or your work in general. With that area of focus in mind, list what you want to achieve in the short and long term. Next, referring to that list, choose the three most important goals. Make those goals specific, measurable, and attainable. Finally, organize those three goals in terms of timelines—one to achieve in the next month, one to achieve in six months, and one to achieve by one year from now. You can list those goals below.

Next month:
Six months:
One year:

REFLECTION:

What do your goals tell you about what you want from your occupation?

How can writing down your goals help you to create a purposeful strategy?

What will you do to make each goal a reality?

DAY 76

BREAK DOWN YOUR GOALS

PURPOSE:

As you learned in yesterday's practice, setting goals can provide clarity and direction. Goal-setting is most effective (and least overwhelming) when you choose goals that are specific and manageable. Writing a 30,000-word book in one month, for instance, seems much more doable when you break it down to 1,000 words per day.

PRACTICE:

Break down each of the three goals you set yesterday. Moving chronologically, list all necessary tasks, projects, people, etc. that will be part of achieving each goal. Use the next page or a separate journal to brainstorm the steps that might be involved in your journey. Next, get organized (and excited!). Order your list, assign due dates, highlight priorities, delegate tasks, and color-code if you want to! Do this for each goal, keeping in mind that it's okay to revise as you go—c'est la vie!

MINDFUL TIP:

Plug your list items into a task- or project-management app for added organization and accountability. Create three different projects (one per goal) and list your tasks for each one. Then do a once-over to ensure that each item starts with a verb (we're talking about action, people!) and that your steps are as specific and actionable as possible.

Remember: a dream with a date becomes a goal, a goal broken down into steps becomes a plan, and a plan backed by action becomes reality.

REFLECTION:

Describe your process for breaking down your goals.

Why is it important to break big goals into small steps?

How will this process help you achieve your goals?

DAY 77

BLOCK YOUR TIME

PURPOSE:

Consider the way you shop for groceries. If you're like most people, you have a list organized by category or section: fresh produce, non-perishables, frozen foods, etc. If you're in the middle of one aisle (or task), you don't generally drop everything to run to another. Time blocking (also called "time chunking") uses the same mentality. Use categorized blocks to manage your time, and you'll find yourself using your time more efficiently.

PRACTICE:

Using the space on the next page or your calendar/scheduling app of choice, write each day of the week, along with its corresponding theme, leaving a few lines in between. Now, consider how you spend your time each day based on your schedule and tasks. List each day's main activities according to when they occur (with task #1 being the first thing in the day). When possible, block similar tasks and activities together.

MINDFUL TIP:

Work within your daily themes as much as you can. For example, schedule errands and bookkeeping on your administrative day, or chunk coaching calls together on a client day. Do what you can to maintain focus, but don't stress if you have a stand-alone activity or task, as this can act as a break between blocks.

REFLECTION:

What did this practice reveal to you about the way you spend your time?

How can time blocking bring focus to your day or week?

How might this process save you time and energy in the long run?

DAY 78

PERSONALIZE YOUR TO-DO LIST

PURPOSE:

Being busy does not necessarily mean being productive. While it's important to have a to-do list that reflects your personal priorities and big-picture goals, be sure to review the list regularly and adapt your list of tasks as needed so you're moving toward what matters most to you.

PRACTICE:

Begin by reviewing previous exercises where you wrote your dreams, priorities, and goals (days 26, 41, and 75). Are the tasks or steps related to these things currently on your to-do list and scheduled into your day? If so, ensure that all your tasks and action steps are specific, organized, and assigned a due date. If they are not, use today as an opportunity to plan your days ahead for success.

MINDFUL TIPS:

- Simplify your to-do list to keep it (and yourself) focused.
- Assign a due date for each task based on your themed days.
- Ensure that each task is specific and actionable.
- Stick to what's important to avoid overloading your list.

REFLECTION:

What personal priorities and big-picture goals do you want your to-do list to reflect?

How will scheduling your dreams, priorities, and goals help you achieve them?

What is the difference between "busy" and "productive?"

DAY 79

IDENTIFY DISTRACTIONS

PURPOSE:

After spending the past few days reviewing, prioritizing, and organizing your time and tasks, you now know how managing these things increases your focus and direction. How you spend your time shapes your whole life; spend it well or others will spend it for you.

PRACTICE:

Repeat after me: "Multitasking is *not* mindful." Commit to doing one thing at a time and doing it well. First, identify what distracts you—social media, office gossip, or compulsively checking your email. Second, schedule these distractions into your day (yes, really); you don't have to completely avoid email or stop talking to your coworkers, but you do need to exercise a bit of schedule discipline. Set a timer or use your distractions as periodic breaks from the work that needs to get done.

REFLECTION:

What are your major distractions?

When will you schedule time for them?

How will you ensure that you get your most important work done without distraction?

DAY 80

CHECK YOUR SCHEDULE

PURPOSE:

Schedules and calendars are essential tools for managing your fixed, flexible, and free time. Scheduling a commitment is a small but crucial step when turning your intention into action. This step brings your ideas out of your head and into your day; it declares, "I commit to investing my time and energy into this activity or person—or myself."

PRACTICE:

First, decide to use either a paper planner or digital calendar. Begin by blocking off your fixed time, then work your way backwards. This might include work hours, meetings, and other scheduled activities. Starting with what you know creates parameters for the rest of your schedule, like building the edges of a puzzle.

Next, arrange your flexible time based on what needs to get done at some point in your day or week (though not necessarily at a specific time). You might consider things like exercise, meal prep, or running errands. The space that remains is your free time to fill (or leave open) as you please. Free time is for family, play, and self-care. Avoid the dangers of hyper-scheduling yourself; leave some blank spots in your day—and keep them blank!

REFLECTION:

How do you want to spend your time and energy?

Does your schedule reflect this? Why or why not?

What priorities or activities do you want to add to your schedule? Where might these fit in?

What do you want to do in your free time?

DAY 81

SET BOUNDARIES

PURPOSE:

Saying "yes" to one thing means saying "no" to another. If you constantly put others first by saying "yes" to their wants and needs before your own, you'll find your priorities pushed so far back that you can barely see them! Setting clear boundaries and expectations—with others and yourself—ensures that you say "yes" to your priorities.

PRACTICE:

Exercise your personal accountability by reflecting on the goals and priorities you've mapped out this past week; keep these visible and let them guide your decisions. For instance, when an opportunity arises, ask yourself if it clearly resonates with your big-picture goals. If it does, you'll know to explore it; if it does not, turn it down.

When you say "no," be polite but firm. Here are some examples of how to kindly but effectively decline:

"Thank you for asking, but I'm unavailable for X."
"I appreciate you thinking of me, but I can't commit to Y."
"Z is my priority, and I feel like X and Y conflict with Z."
"Thank you, but I have to decline."

REFLECTION:

Where do you want to spend your energy?

What might be an example of a "good opportunity" (one that aligns with your priorities)?

How will you know when to say "no?"

How will you steer clear of distractions or conflicting opportunities?

DAY 82

ELIMINATE THE UNNECESSARY

PURPOSE:

Being productive does not mean doing everything—it means doing the right things that bring you closer to your big-picture wants, needs, and goals. Un-busy yourself by recognizing which tasks are unnecessary, or which may be more appropriate for someone else to handle. This way, you can invest more of your time into doing what's really important.

PRACTICE:

Create a specific plan for time-sucking tasks that have little ROI (return on investment). Here are a few examples:

- Deal with lurking to-do list tasks: for each item, decide to do it, delegate it, or delete it.

- Block social media sites during work hours or work offline.

- Check email once in the morning, after lunch, and near the end of your workday.

MINDFUL TIPS:

- Set boundaries and deadlines to prevent (or at least combat) procrastination.
- Reward yourself after you've done X amount of work, rather than after X amount of time.
- Tidy your desk and organize physical and digital folders.
- Ask others to hold you accountable.

REFLECTION:

How did you eliminate unnecessary distractions?

How did the steps you took today increase your mental and physical space?

How can this exercise help you in other areas of your life?

DAY 83

SEEK GUIDANCE

PURPOSE:

Your future is a worthy investment. Wherever you want to learn, grow, or gain success, seeking guidance from an expert can simplify and expedite your process. Learning from someone else's gains, losses, and lessons can save you a lot of time, energy, money, and stress in the long run. Plus, connecting with someone who will hold you accountable to your goals and priorities ensures that you stay focused and moving in the right direction.

PRACTICE:

Contemplate today's reflection questions. Let your answer to the last question determine your next steps.

REFLECTION:

What kind of guidance aligns with your goals, values, and priorities (e.g., business consulting, life coaching, relationship counseling, financial advice, etc.)?

Whose mentorship might you benefit from? Why?

What time, energy, and financial investment would this require you to make?

Do you think this investment is worth the guidance you will receive? Why or why not?

DAY 84

CREATE A PROCESS

PURPOSE:

Most people have their eyes on the prize, but they get stuck on how to attain it. Identifying the steps of your "how" (and knowing them inside-out) helps you approach your work with clarity and purpose. This approach leads you to the results you want to see—in work and in life.

PRACTICE:

Start with one result you want to see in your work or workday. Identify your target, then determine the change(s) you'll need to make. What steps will you need to take to actualize these changes? For instance, if you want to get your email inbox to zero by Friday at 5 p.m. so you can relax over the weekend, you'll need a process to organize, automate, and declutter your email. Here are some suggestions of steps you might include in that process:

- Organize emails into categorized folders based on daily themes, projects, or tasks.

- Avoid lingering messages by turning them into to-do list tasks or calendar appointments.

- Unsubscribe from unnecessary lists and set up a separate email account for subscriptions.

MINDFUL TIP:

Make your process specific and actionable so you can reach your target, and ensure that it is simple enough to start today.

REFLECTION:

What results do you want to see in your work or workday?

What process did you create today to lead you closer to those results?

Which other areas of your life would benefit from a simple, purposeful process?

DAY 85

TRACK YOUR MONEY

PURPOSE:

By this point, you've gained clarity on where and how you want to invest your time and energy. Now is a key time to check whether your financial investments reflect your intentions. Do you put your money where your mouth—or heart—is? Your financial investments shape your mindset, choices, and lifestyle; keeping track of these holds you accountable to your priorities and sets Future You up for long-term success and wellbeing.

PRACTICE:

Create a spreadsheet or use a budgeting app to track your spending. Start by plugging in what's consistent—for example, your income and regular expenses. As you go about your day, track your expenditures (e.g., fuel, groceries, online courses, coaching, eating out, leisure activities, etc.) to gain a better understanding of the investments you're making.

REFLECTION:

Do your current spending habits reflect the priorities and goals you've set for yourself? Why or why not?

How can tracking your money lead you to invest in what's important to you?

What changes do you need to make to your spending habits/ financial investments?

DAY 86

TAKE A BREAK

PURPOSE:

After too much time or repetition, your brain switches from active to passive mode in order to conserve energy (and perhaps a bit of sanity). This shift into autopilot slowly diminishes your perceived importance of the task at hand. Taking a break allows you to return to your task with renewed energy, purpose, and concentration.

PRACTICE:

Work in intervals today by taking a five-minute break every hour. Choose your task, set a timer, and do your thing. When the timer goes off, leave your work area (I repeat, *clear the area!*). Stretch, practice deep breathing, or get some fresh air. Pay attention to your mindset and energy levels when you return to your task.

REFLECTION:

How did taking regular breaks positively impact your workday?

How did it affect your energy, mindset, and emotions?

What will you do to remind yourself to take regular breaks?

DAY 87

PRACTICE CREATIVITY

PURPOSE:

Great inventions and innovations begin with one question: "What if...?" This eventually leads to, "Hey, I have a crazy idea!" which seems absolutely impossible—until it *isn't*. The creative process requires something we rarely allow ourselves: time and mental space to indulge our curiosity and play with ideas.

PRACTICE:

Make time for creative brainstorming today. How can you implement a strategy you've always wanted to try? How can you reframe a problem into a question, or approach something from a different angle? Choose your focus area and write or record your ideas—no matter how silly or impossible they seem. See what you can come up with when you embrace the far-fetched, without pressure to think of something perfect right off the bat. (You can sift through your list afterwards and expand on your favorite ideas.)

REFLECTION:

How did this exercise of creative brainstorming benefit you?

What made it challenging?

How might you use a creative approach in other aspects of your work and personal life?

DAY 88

EXPLORE COLLABORATION

PURPOSE:

Collaboration is a wonderful way to learn from others' insight and expertise. There are countless people doing extraordinary things in all facets of work and life! Rather than viewing them as competition, explore ways to collaborate and learn from one another. You may be surprised how much farther you can go with the support of others.

PRACTICE:

Create an opportunity for collaboration. What projects or ideas do you have that might benefit from someone else's involvement? What opportunities do others have to offer? Explore ways to build connections with like-minded people, and reach out to those people today.

REFLECTION:

Whose work or mindset do you admire?

Who have you always wanted to work with?

What ideas do you have for collaborative projects?

DAY 89

REVAMP YOUR WORKSPACE

PURPOSE:

Most people spend around a third of their day at work. Whether you have a physical or digital workplace, make your space as pleasant as possible. Your environment affects you on a physical, emotional, mental, and sometimes even spiritual level, so keep it clean, organized, and inspiring.

PRACTICE:

Start by making your space functional and manageable. Declutter and organize your office, desk, and devices. This will improve your productivity and wellbeing by minimizing stress and distractions. Next, spruce things up! Invite into your space what you want to see in your work. If you want creativity and inspiration, for instance, try adding a plant, new accessory, or piece of art to your space. Transforming where you work can bring a new, positive energy into how you work.

REFLECTION:

What qualities do you want your work to reflect?

What did you bring into your space to invite this kind of focus or energy?

How did transforming your space help you connect to and enjoy the work you create within it?

DAY 90

PREPARE YOURSELF

PURPOSE:

Your thoughts and beliefs set the stage for your immediate actions and ongoing habits. Making a specific plan to move toward your goals and dreams provides the clarity and confidence you need to achieve your version of success. Focus today on preparing yourself for what you want as though it's entirely possible (or even inevitable!) and is already on its way to you.

PRACTICE:

Think about the big-picture goals and dreams you identified earlier in this section and throughout this book (see days 26, 41, and 75). Write down the ones that continue to strike a chord with you and ask yourself what your life will look like when—not *if*, but *when*—you attain your goal or manifest your dream.

Repeat this process with each goal or dream using the format: "When I _____ my life will look like _____."

Once you've completed this process for each goal, dream, and desire, map out your reflection questions.

REFLECTION:

Since that life is already waiting for you, what are three ways you can prepare for it?

1.

2.

3.

What are your next steps?

CHAPTER FIVE REFLECTION

Take a moment to reflect on the past 18 days and the commitment you have made to becoming aware of your occupation.

How have you learned to set meaningful goals and manage your time to pursue your priorities?

Which practices resonated with you? Make a note of those you want to come back to.

Before moving forward:

- Be proud of the investment you've made in yourself.

- Recognize the insight you have gained because of the work you've done.

- Celebrate the growth you've experienced because you chose to grow.

- Remember your capacity for self-empowerment, fulfillment, and transformation.

- Believe that you will continue to connect to your inner wisdom should you choose to live with mindfulness.

CHAPTER SIX: NETWORK

"Go out into the world today and love the people you meet. Let your presence light new light in the hearts of people."

—MOTHER TERESA

DAY 91

IDENTIFY YOUR CONNECTIONS

PURPOSE:

Knowing you are part of a larger network is powerful. This knowledge can help you gain confidence and practice gratitude as you recognize your supports, as well as the impact you have on others. Identifying your meaningful connections also helps you challenge the myth that investing in yourself is selfish; when you're aware of your connections, you can see exactly who you impact and how.

PRACTICE:

Map out your connections by creating a web of those most important to you.

1. Grab a piece of paper and begin by writing and circling your name in the center of the page.
2. Write each group or network that you're part of in its own circle on the page: family, friends, work, sports team, book club, etc.
3. Create a web of connections by drawing a line from your name to each circle. For your strongest or most important networks, you might draw a bold line (or two).

4. Next, expand each network's circle into its own web to include the names of specific people you want to recognize.
5. Highlight the names of those you feel most connected to.
6. Add any other important connections to your page and take a moment to give gratitude for your connections.

MINDFUL TIP:

Remember that this exercise is for you to acknowledge the connections that are important to you. There is no pressure to include anyone you don't want to!

REFLECTION:

Take a moment to acknowledge and appreciate the strong connections in your life. How do these connections make your life better?

What can you do to invest in these important relationships?

DAY 92

MAKE YOURSELF AVAILABLE

PURPOSE:

You make time for what (and who) is important to you. Valuing your relationship with someone—whether a friend, family member, or significant other—means sharing time with them. Opening yourself (and your schedule) to someone is the only way the relationship will grow deeper and stronger.

PRACTICE:

Reach out to someone whose presence enriches your life. Whether they add laughter, meaning, or other inspiration, connect with this fantastic person and set up a time for the two of you to meet up. Open your schedule to make yourself available, and follow through when the time comes to get together (I can't stress this enough!). If you consistently flake out on someone, they're not going to feel valued!

MINDFUL TIP:

If you struggle with following through, ask yourself what hurdles you face and why. Consider what each hurdle might tell you about your needs, priorities, and boundaries.

REFLECTION:

Who did you connect with today?

How and why did you commit to making yourself available to this person?

How will you overcome any hurdles you might face with following through on commitments?

DAY 93

EXPRESS GRATITUDE

PURPOSE:

Being truly grateful for someone is a beautiful thing that can make you feel warm and fuzzy inside. Sharing your gratitude gives those warm fuzzies to someone else, which can transform their entire day, not to mention their self-perception and relationship with you. This practice also benefits *you;* expressing gratitude fosters a positive mindset (you see the good in others) and an open heart (you feel the joy and richness their presence adds to your life). You might even lead that person to think about and share why they're grateful for *you.*

PRACTICE:

Reflect on the connections you mapped out on day 91. Visit or call one person today for the sole purpose of expressing your gratitude. Be specific as to why they mean so much to you. Let that be the first thing you share (without complaining or asking them to help you move!).

REFLECTION:

Who did you call?

What did you express gratitude for?

How did this experience make you feel?

How did the other person respond?

How might expressing gratitude benefit your other relationships?

DAY 94

RECONNECT WITH A FRIEND

PURPOSE:

Some friendships naturally stagnate when people move away or go down different paths. Other times, friendships fade from years of neglect, carelessness, or lack of follow-through. It's important to recognize the current condition of the relationships you value and to engage in those you want to maintain.

PRACTICE:

Think about a friend or connection you've drifted away from. Reach out to this person today to retell a shared story, express gratitude for their friendship, or simply touch base to let them know you're thinking about them.

MINDFUL TIP:

This is not an invitation to rekindle an unhealthy relationship from the past. Reach out to someone who was and will be a positive influence in your life.

REFLECTION:

Who did you reach out to?

Why is this person's friendship valuable to you?

What does this reveal to you about the characteristics you value in friends?

DAY 95

SEND A LETTER

PURPOSE:

Taking time to express thoughts and feelings of gratitude in a handwritten letter benefits both the one writing the letter (that's you!) and the person reading it. Not only will this exercise deepen your appreciation for the person you're writing to, but it will also brighten their day to receive something in their mailbox that isn't a bill or flyer. Hooray!

PRACTICE:

Choose one person to write to: a parent, partner, friend, mentor, etc. In your *handwritten* letter, thank this person and let them know how much you value their presence in your life. And please remember to actually *mail* your letter!

REFLECTION:

Who did you write to?

What did you thank this person for?

How did this exercise make you feel about your relationship with this person?

Who else might you write to in the future?

DAY 96

DO SOMETHING KIND

PURPOSE:

Small acts of kindness are done with one intention: love. Kindness spreads love, and love makes everything brighter. Doing something kind for someone else lights up their world while also adding a little sparkle to your own. Remember that you invite into your life what you give to the world around you. Get into the habit of giving and inviting love.

PRACTICE:

Go out of your way today to do something kind for someone you know. Surprise your friend, coworker, or significant other simply because you want that person to have a better day. Let go of any expectation that your kind deed will be reciprocated. Practice kindness with only one intention: to share love.

REFLECTION:

What was your act of kindness today?

How did this act share love with another person?

How did this practice make you feel?

What did it show you about your ability to impact someone else and the world around you?

DAY 97

HELP A STRANGER

PURPOSE:

Kindness and happiness only grow when shared. Taking a small step out of your day to bring joy and offer support to another person could mean the world to them. It might even start a chain reaction! As a human being, you are part of an interwoven network of people who need love and connection. Everyone has something to offer and to learn; we might as well work together.

PRACTICE:

Do something kind for someone you don't know. Pay for their coffee, offer a genuine compliment, or strike up an honest conversation with a stranger. Carry on yesterday's practice of finding a way to spread love without the expectation that your kind deed will be reciprocated.

MINDFUL TIP:

Before you leave your house today, tell yourself that you will do something nice for a stranger. Keeping this intention in mind will lead your brain to seek out opportunities to help.

REFLECTION:

What did you do to help a stranger today?

How did this act share love or brighten their day?

How did this practice make you feel?

What did it show you about your ability to make an impact on someone and to the world around you?

DAY 98

BE PRESENT

PURPOSE:

In order to build lasting friendships of value, you've got to be present and engaged during your time together. Building a mindful relationship means putting your phones and other distractions aside, getting to know one another, and being present in each other's company.

PRACTICE:

Remember that commitment you made almost a week ago (day 92) to make yourself available to a friend or loved one? If you haven't already followed through on this, today is your lucky day! (If you have, that's fantastic! Let's do it again.)

Get together with your friend before the day is done. Grab a snack, go for a walk, hit up a yoga class, or share in another healthy activity. Make sure you've dealt with any potential distractions beforehand so that you can commit to a mindful interaction with your friend. You can even request a "no-phone zone" while you hang out.

REFLECTION:

Reflect on the time you spent with your friend.
What made it valuable?

How did you stay present and engaged?

What can you do to be more present when spending time with others?

DAY 99

ASK FOR HELP

PURPOSE:

It can be daunting to ask someone else for help (especially if you're used to being the helper). Vulnerability is essential to your wellbeing, as well as that of your relationships. Oftentimes, the hardest part of this process is getting out of your own way (or head) and allowing someone to support you. Vulnerability shows that you're human—and it invites reciprocity, which is key to a balanced relationship.

PRACTICE:

How might you benefit from someone else's guidance, insight, or accountability? Reach out to someone you trust and ask them to listen, offer advice, or support you in another way.

REFLECTION:

Who did you reach out to today and why?

How did your vulnerability benefit your relationship with this person?

What did you find challenging about being vulnerable and asking for help?

How do you benefit from practicing vulnerability and inviting reciprocity in your relationships?

DAY 100

OFFER YOUR TIME

PURPOSE:

You know by now that you are part of an interconnected network of individuals, and that helping others creates a ripple effect of love throughout this network. An important question to keep asking yourself is, "How can I contribute?" Your contribution has the power to spread ripples of love, while also giving you a sense of purpose and belonging.

PRACTICE:

Yesterday, you bravely asked for (and hopefully received) support from someone else. Today's practice invites reciprocity as you contribute your most precious resource: time. Look for a specific way to offer your time to a friend, group, or community. Ask yourself what role you can play, or simply ask someone what you can do to help.

REFLECTION:

How can you offer your time, energy, or skills to someone or something you value?

Why is it important to you to help this person or cause?

How does the practice of contribution offer you a sense of purpose and belonging?

DAY 101

KEEP GOOD COMPANY

PURPOSE:

You now have a better understanding of who you are and what you value. Do your friendships bring you closer to the person you want to be? Do they empower you to pursue your dreams and live out your values? Remember that the people you surround yourself with can shape your perspectives, character, and entire life. Choose these people with care.

PRACTICE:

Create distance from those who invite drama or negativity into your life. (You don't have to completely cut ties if you don't want to, but start by separating yourself from these folks today.) Instead, spend time with positive, supportive people whose company brings you joy. Invest your energy into the people who deserve it.

REFLECTION:

Who did you choose to distance yourself from today? Why?

Who did you choose to spend time with today?

In what ways do they add to your life?

How do you define "good company?"

DAY 102

FIND YOUR PEOPLE

PURPOSE:

Humanity is a massive, interconnected web, and you are connected to everyone within it. Knowing and believing this can provide a profound sense of comfort and belonging within a seemingly chaotic world. You might also find it encouraging to know that you are already connected to the people you want to meet; you simply need to reach out and build that personal connection.

PRACTICE:

Yesterday, you practiced being selective about the company you keep. Now, consider the kind of people you want to bring into your circle. Who can you reach out to today? Contact someone you admire or would like to connect with. Sign up to be part of an interesting group. Post on social media that you're seeking like-minded people to collaborate with. Make the first move.

REFLECTION:

Identify or describe the person you want to connect with.

What draws you to this person?

What does your connection look like?

Why is this connection important to you?

Who did (or will) you reach out to in order to build this connection?

DAY 103

TRANSFORM SMALL TALK

PURPOSE:

Every moment of your day is a chance to transform the ordinary into the extraordinary. Maybe that's a bit cliché, but there are plenty of ways to add depth and meaning into your routine. Challenge yourself to see mundane tasks and responsibilities as opportunities for connection (yes, even small talk). You never know what kind of conversation you might spark.

PRACTICE:

Focus on creating memorable interactions by humanizing your conversations today. Respond to "How are you?" by recounting a positive story or sharing something personal. Answer "What do you do?" with a list of hobbies and activities, rather than the usual description of your job title.

If you're up for a challenge, make it your mission to ask someone else a meaningful question:

"What are you passionate about?"
"Why did you choose to do that job?"
"What are you grateful for today?"

REFLECTION:

Describe your extraordinary interaction(s). What happened when you asked and/or answered ordinary questions in a meaningful way?

How did you build connection through this practice?

How can transforming small talk transform the way you perceive and interact with others?

DAY 104

VOCALIZE YOUR GRATITUDE

PURPOSE:

You know from previous practices that gratitude is most useful and abundant when shared. This is especially true when it's shared in a meaningful way (e.g., verbally instead of texting heart emojis). Not only does this have the power to deepen your relationships, but it also gets you in the transformative practice of identifying and communicating your gratitude.

PRACTICE:

Meet with or call someone you're grateful for today. During your conversation, tell that person you are thankful for them—not just because of what they've done for you but for who they are as a person. Feel free to use one or more of the following statements to share your appreciation:

"I am grateful for your presence in my life."
"I appreciate who you are."
"Your friendship has made my life better because _____."
"I think you're a wonderful person because _____."

REFLECTION:

Who did you call or meet with?

How did that person respond to your gratitude?

How did this practice make you feel?

What did you learn about your relationships and yourself?

DAY 105

PHONE A FRIEND

PURPOSE:

How tiresome is it to check your phone 20 times a day while pouring your heart out to a friend over text? Relieve your thumbs, neck, and attention span and give that person a call! Make time for meaningful interactions with the people who make time for you.

PRACTICE:

Pick one person you frequently text and give them a call to check in, catch up, and let them know you care. Be sure to set aside enough time for a meaningful conversation or offer to arrange a time that works for both of you.

MINDFUL TIP:

Your phone call might also be a great time to practice other exercises from this chapter.

REFLECTION:

Who did you call today?

How did this phone call benefit your relationship?

If applicable: What other exercise did you practice during your phone call? What happened?

DAY 106

SHARE IN WONDER

PURPOSE:

The overwhelm of routine and responsibility can lead you to forget about or lose interest in the world around you. Acknowledging and appreciating the beauty in your surroundings gives you a fresh perspective of gratitude and wonder. This practice also plays a major role in cultivating personal fulfillment.

PRACTICE:

Go on a local adventure with a friend and search for three things that bring you joy, wonder, or fulfillment. Look for cool events, natural wonders, local art, or something the two of you have in common. You can even pretend that you're tourists who have just set foot in your city, town, or neighborhood. Check online reviews, ask locals what places are worth seeing, or simply walk around and create your own adventure. Have fun and make a day of it!

REFLECTION:

Write your three wonders below.

1.

2.

3.

How did this exercise help you connect to your surroundings?

What was it like to share your joy or wonder with someone else?

How does searching for what you want to see make you more ready to find it?

DAY 107

PLAY YOUR PART

PURPOSE:

Throughout this book, you've found and created multiple opportunities to make the world shine brighter through kindness and gratitude. Now it's time to scale your efforts and abilities by reaching even deeper into your powerful inner wisdom and potential. You have an important gift to share with the world that only you can give, and you share this gift by being aware of and aligned with your true self. Aligning with what makes you authentically you is how you improve the world inside you and around you.

PRACTICE:

Make time to connect with your true self today. First, identify when or where you feel most open, aware, aligned, and/or peaceful. What thoughts or practices bring you closer to this truth inside of you? With this knowledge and intention, repeat a previous practice that aligns with this truth. It might be something you found enjoyable, meditative, or enlightening. Dig deep to find what feels most like you, and remember: the fact that you want to tap into your true self means that you are already moving in the right direction.

REFLECTION:

In what way(s) did you align with your true self today?

What does this version of you feel like?

How else can you connect with yourself?

DAY 108

SHINE YOUR LIGHT

PURPOSE:

In the past 108 days, you explored the wisdom and potential within you. You began to recognize and align with your capacity for empowerment, fulfillment, and transformation, and you shared your learning with others through daily practice. As you continue to integrate mindfulness into your everyday life, you will invite positive change into the lives of those around you. Cultivate the light within you, and you will light the path for others.

PRACTICE:

This final practice is your call to action to help others cultivate mindfulness as you continue to grow your own. Tell everyone you know (and those you don't) what you've learned and how you've grown. Better yet, show them what mindfulness looks like by living out what you now know to be true for yourself, and share this book with anyone who might benefit from its messages and practices.

REFLECTION:

How will you continue to shine your light?

How will you light the path for others?

CHAPTER SIX REFLECTION

Take a moment to reflect on the past 18 days and the commitment you have made to become aware of your network.

How have you nourished relationships that deepen your sense of belonging?

Which practices resonated with you? Make a note of those you want to come back to.

And now, let me congratulate you on completing the final exercise of this book! Think about all you have created and become in 108 days. You are a more aware, authentic, and complete version of yourself, and I am so proud of you for sticking to your practice.

Before moving forward:

- Be proud of the investment you've made in yourself.
- Recognize the insight you have gained because of the work you've done.
- Celebrate the growth you've experienced because you chose to grow.
- Remember your capacity for self-empowerment, fulfillment, and transformation.
- Believe that you will continue to connect to your inner wisdom should you choose to live with mindfulness.

CONCLUSION

At the beginning of this book, I expressed my hope that you would do and experience three things:

1. Recognize your worth and live according to it.
2. Truly appreciate the beauty of your existence.
3. Trust in your ability to create fulfilling changes in your life and yourself.

You have taken 108 steps toward each of these goals, and you have moved toward a wonderful transformation. It's important for you to remember that your transformation came from within. These practices may have provided guidance through your process of self-realization, but *you* did the work. Let's take a moment to acknowledge and celebrate the incredible work you've done within yourself:

- You trained yourself to reconnect with your body and listen to what it tells you.

- You navigated through deep, uncomfortable feelings and learned how to trust yourself.

- You practiced observing and reframing your thoughts to gain clarity and control.

- You asked tough questions to explore your spirituality and personal truth.

- You set meaningful goals and managed your time to pursue your priorities.

- And finally, you connected with others and built healthy, empowering relationships.

You awakened to your inner wisdom and potential, and, in doing so, you created meaningful changes in your life and self. That was the purpose of these 108 days; let that be the purpose of your days going forward.

You have a unique and important gift to share with the world. Only you hold this gift, and therefore only you can share it. To do so, you must remain aware of, aligned with, and authentic to your true self. The work you've done here has built your foundation, but these past 108 days were only the beginning. Living a mindful life and living in accordance with your truth requires an ongoing commitment to yourself and to the wisdom and potential within you. Sticking to this commitment will demand your time, attention, vulnerability, and trust.

Trust yourself amid distractions. Trust that you have the capacity for your empowerment, fulfillment, and transformation. And trust that the world will be receptive to what you have to offer.

Above all else, trust in your truth and live in accordance with it. This is what it means to be fully awake and in alignment. It is your path to yourself, your inner wisdom, and your fulfillment. And it is how you create meaningful changes in the world around you.

By connecting to the wisdom within, you awaken, empower, and fulfill your true self. Live mindfully in alignment with this truth, and you will share your gift with the world. The world is ready to receive it.

ABOUT THE AUTHOR

Melissa Steginus is a mindfulness teacher and productivity coach who helps people structure their work and lives to be intentional, empowering, and fulfilling. With a background in social work and years of experience as a counselor, coach, yoga instructor, business strategist, and entrepreneur, she has helped thousands of people transform their personal and professional lives through her workshops, classes, online courses, and individual sessions.

Melissa lives blissfully on the west coast of Canada, where she offers coaching and workshops on mindfulness, stress reduction, and intentional productivity for entrepreneurs, business owners, and students of all ages. You can discover more and sign up for her newsletter at melissasteginus.com.

CONNECT WITH MELISSA STEGINUS

Sign up for Melissa's newsletter at:
www.melissasteginus.com/subscribe

To find out more information visit her website:
www.melissasteginus.com

Social media:
www.facebook.com/melissasteginusonline
www.instagram.com/melissasteginus
www.twitter.com/melissasteginus

Other published works:
www.amzn.to/2oYs0e3

BOOK DISCOUNTS AND SPECIAL DEALS

Get discounts and special deals on books at
www.TCKpublishing.com/bookdeals

This book comes with free mindfulness resources, worksheets, and exercises to help you transform your life.

Get your resources at:
www.melissasteginus.com/mindful

Made in the USA
Middletown, DE
23 November 2020

24891523R00139